MW01172913

Doing Good

While Doing Well™

How real estate investors provide a service and make a difference

By

Lou Brown

&

Local Certified Affordable Housing Providers

Table of Contents

Introduction

Welcome to the first day of the rest of your life! I say that, knowing that many of you reading this are embarking on a new journey. Real estate is brand-new and foreign to you. And you are getting involved for one important reason – financial freedom for yourself and your family.

Perhaps you are like so many others that have seen what the corporate world can do and realized an important axiom (and one that I have lived my life by) – "If it is to be, it is up to me!"

What's surprising to many people is that making money in real estate is like any other business- It's based on a formula. Those who have failed in real estate have failed because they did not follow a known proven business model – which is nothing more than a formula. They followed their own plan. And as far as I'm concerned, running a business without a model is like building a house without blueprints.

If you look at my track record in the real estate industry, you will see that I am known as an innovator. If something is not working in the real estate industry, I like to look at it from all angles, tear it apart, see what does and does not work, then put it back together again – only this time in a way that will actually work.

I applaud those of you who have made the decision to move forward in real estate investing, even though some of you reading this are still filled with a little bit of fear and apprehension. That's ok. It's normal. Do you think my first business deal went smoothly? No, baby! Going out on your own into an unknown business has the slightest possibility that you could fail and lose everything you worked so hard for. But it's not a reason to give up before you even try. My colleagues and I will be showing and proving that this fear can be overcome by proven solutions that already exist.

Doing Good While Doing Well

For example, what if I could show and tell you that with X amount of investment you can get X amount of leads that will yield X amount of deals that will yield XX amount of profit? That's a pretty profound statement, yet it is true. In fact, it's somewhat magical.

But before that can happen, obtaining the right education and tools is critical. Think about college - they don't just deliver a diploma after you've paid the big fat check. First, you have to get the recommended textbooks and go through a number of classes. Then and only then can you move to the business world and seek a job in your chosen profession. The sad thing is, even with all the studying and diploma, most people do not end up with a long-term job in their chosen arena.

In business, there is a short circuit to the whole process. It's called a franchise. Someone else has already been there, done that, proven the straight path to the money, and has developed a plan that allows others to follow that path - and boy, does that make all the difference!

It's pretty profound and one that works for a lot of people - but the franchisee must apply the tools and education they have been given in order to be successful.

Over time, that is what has been developed in real estate. The Certified Affordable Housing Provider® program is designed to short-circuit the process of learning the who, what, where, when, and how of making money in real estate.

Join me now as you meet other people who are just like you – they wanted a better life than the one they had! Simply put - they wanted a better life. They liked the concept of 'Doing Good While Doing Well™' and committed to following the formula to attain sustainable success.

At the end of this book, I'm going to invite you to do the same! See you at the top!

Best, Lou

Chapter 1

Doing Good While Doing Well

By Lou Brown

"If it is to be - it is up to me!"

Our business inspires me!

That's a rare statement for a lot of business owners to make. But for me, it is absolutely true. I think back to when I was a kid. There are two distinct things I remember from my childhood. Money was tough, and I really had no one to fall back on.

My mom had made some bad decisions about life partners, and it ended up being just her and me against the world. Now, this was back in the day when there were not a lot of government programs to help out. I'm not sure, but I don't think it would've mattered. My mother was proud and did not really want or seek help from others.

You see, my mom was from Scotland. She came over as a war bride, and all of her family was in Scotland. We were estranged from my father, and hence, his entire family. So that just left us.

I know what it's like to have no money. I know what it's like to hide out from the rent man. My mom would say, "shhh, don't say anything... I'll have the money by this weekend." She just didn't want to face anyone and have to say that.

Now I didn't know it then, but the universe was starting its alignment with my journey in life.

I never will forget the one time we went to see some of her friends. I called them aunts and uncles, as I had none. I was about eight years old, and Aunt Mabel told me a story. She said they had just bought the duplex they lived in. She told me they went to the bank, got a loan, and that the people on the other side were paying enough money in rent the cover the mortgage. What did she just say?? Even at that age I realized what she said was that they were living there for free!!

Can you imagine how that captured my imagination? Now, of course, I didn't know anything about finances or money or how other people even lived. The one thing I did know was - *we* didn't have the money for rent sometimes, and *she* didn't have to pay any.

That's probably where I got the first insight that there really are parallel universes out there. Some people struggle with money, and others don't. Some people put forth the effort to think and educate themselves and uncover truths that are unknown to those who do not.

Wow! So all I have to do is remember that there are people fortunate enough to apply themselves and, in return, get pieces of information that allow them to break the money code.

The Money Code

The money code is quite fascinating. I am definitely a student of it. Some people work their entire lives and end up with very little to show for it, while others seem to effortlessly move through life and always have plenty of money to spend. So, what's the difference?

I recall that my mother (God rest her soul) was one of the ones who did not take the time or gain the tools to master money -Money mastered her. I did not like the process and saw how high interest on borrowed money could eat a fortune in a hurry.

So I watched and studied the processes involved. We visited Aunt Mabel, and she told us she had bought the duplex next door and that the people on that side were paying enough in rent to cover the mortgage, with enough left over to go into their pockets. I watched their lifestyle change: a new Cadillac every other year, nice furniture, trips, and cruises. And they ate out at the steakhouse almost every night!

They just kept buying real estate. One day, Aunt Mabel called me and asked me to help her move. They had just bought a brand-new house. It was a two-story, all brick home, in a brand-new subdivision, on a corner lot. Far more house than she, Uncle George, and their two Chihuahuas needed.

"How did you do this, Mabel?" was my question. She said two words that changed my life: **Accumulate Property.**

Now, this parallel universe continued. When I was about 12 years old, my mother heard about a program that would allow us to buy a home. It was a modest three-bedroom home. It was very exciting, and things looked positive. Then form after form was completed and time passed, we were told that she did not qualify.

This devastated her. She didn't say much, but I could tell it really took the wind out of her sails. It was something that she wanted for me. She wanted me out of those apartments – those terrible apartments – and get me into something better, more room, a better location, and in turn, a better life.

That was not to be. It affected her so badly that she never tried again.

Several years later, when I was about 18 years, old Aunt Mabel said to me, "hey, you need to buy a house." I said, "yeah, that would be nice, Aunt Mabel, but you've bought all your property by qualifying for loans. I can't qualify my way out of a paper bag."

She laughed and said I needed to meet her friend 'Realtor Sue.' One phone call and realtor Sue was anxious to show me some property. You see, I had worked very hard during my teenage years. I had first started a paper route when I was 11 years old (actually, I was not supposed to start till 12, but I fibbed a bit.) I wanted to get ahead, and I figured this was a chance.

Every chance I got, I saved up money and worked after-school jobs, and did other things to make things work. And I knew one thing – I wanted a better life for myself and my mom.

It didn't take long until realtor Sue found a house that I liked. Turns out, I could buy this house differently than Aunt Mabel did.

Again I discovered a parallel universe: those who go to banks and qualify for loans and buy property, versus those who buy property a different way.

And the second way made all the difference.

Essentially.... it's to use the seller as the bank.

I ended up buying my first property at the age of 19 without even going to a bank or qualifying for a loan. That was a real eye-opener!

My mother became my first tenant, paying me $100 per month (along with washing some clothes and cooking some meals. ☺) It was a good deal for me because it helped make ends meet, but it was also a good deal for her. Our rent was about $600 per month, and I told her to take $500 per month and put it towards her debt. Within a year and a half, she was debt-free for the rest of her life. That was a new experience for her.

I got to see first-hand that if my mother had discovered this other universe when I was 12 years old, then I would not have spent my teenage years in an apartment.

Knowledge is power. In fact, I teach that 'Knowledge is Power *and Money*.'

As time passed, I was transferred by the company I worked for from Charlotte, North Carolina, to Atlanta, Georgia. Why not? My mom was all set and the company offered to pay my closing costs if I would sell my house and buy a new one down there. So I did, and in the process, I was surprised to see that in less than two years, my property had gone up by 37%!

In Atlanta, I again decided not to qualify for a loan, even though I could have. I told the agent to find me a house where the seller would be the bank.

Once again it happened, and to this day I have **never** qualified for a loan from a bank for a single-family or small multifamily property. There was - and is - no reason to. Why would I?

I also started to realize that if I offered my real estate the same way to the people who wanted to live there, then I could help change their lives as well. Why should they be relegated to being renters for the rest of their lives?

I could become the bank for them as the seller and give them what I would eventually call "The Path to Home Ownership®."

Inspiration

I started this story with "Our Business Inspires Me!" Likely now you can understand why I think so. Imagine working with a couple or a family and showing them that there is another way.

Imagine giving them a leg up in life and an opportunity that no one else has given them. Imagine working with them to help them improve their credit to the point that they can get a new loan. Or just be the bank for them and give them pride of ownership and the opportunity of possibility.

I have so many stories of people we have helped. One was a 63 years old gentleman who had never owned a home in his name in his life. He started out with our *Work for Equity Program* and did all the repairs to the home with the help of his family and friends. We credited that work towards his down payment. This allowed him the opportunity to work with a credit repair program and get his credit cleaned up so that he could get a new bank loan.

Doing Good While Doing Well

Another success story was a nurse. She loved the idea of our *Work for Equity Program* and even though she didn't have a lot of experience, she went to training sessions at the local builder supply store and learned how to do her own tile and sheetrock work. She transformed her home and made it look absolutely beautiful. We became the bank for her and have been her bank for over five years now.

We also have a couple in the Chattanooga, Tennessee area that lived in a mobile home on her father's land for over 20 years. We had a beautiful home available on 5 acres of land and have become the bank for these nice people for the past four years.

The stories are endless, and the challenges that human beings face are much more intense than I had to face.

People who are selling their homes are drawn to our program. They see that the home that they have enjoyed and raised their children in can be passed along through our process to a deserving family who will be raising their family there, while helping the community as well.

Whether you are a buyer, seller, lender, or real estate investor, you can likely see how it makes perfect sense to work with - and be inspired by - a Certified Affordable Housing Provider® offering the *Path To Home Ownership®* program.

Join me now and become inspired by people from throughout this country who are changing lives and making a difference in the world by 'Doing Good While Doing Well™.'

About Lou Brown

Investors have long regarded the training, systems and forms created by **Louis "Lou" Brown** as the best in the industry. Quoted as an expert by many publications such as *The Wall Street Journal* and *Smart Money,* Lou draws from his wide and varied background as a real estate investor. Having bought property since 1977, he has invested in single-family homes, apartments, hotels, and developed subdivisions, as well as building and renovating homes and apartments. These experiences have given him a proving ground for the most cutting-edge concepts in the real estate investment industry today. He is widely known as a creative financing genius regarding his deal structuring concepts. He enjoys sharing his discoveries with others as he teaches seminars and has authored courses, books and audio training on how to make money and keep it.

Lou is past President and a lifetime member of the Georgia Real Estate Investors Association and was founding President of the National Real Estate Investors Association. He firmly believes that the path to success is through ongoing education and invests thousands of dollars annually in his own.

Lou loves to spend time in Atlanta with his beautiful wife Janice, their two children and foster daughter, and he always makes time to speak with other realtors and investors about his *Street Smart* and *Path to Homeownership* programs.

So if you are interested in learning how Lou can take you to the next level, then visit his website at **www.louisbrown.com** or contact him directly at **StreetSmartLouis@LouisBrown.com**.

Doing Good While Doing Well

Street Smart Systems, LLC

Chapter 1

Why Second Chances Matter

Kevin Margo and Amy Selmek

Kevin: My start in the real estate business began in 1993. I purchased a home for my family, and the property happened to have another small home on it.

We rented the smaller home out and used the extra income to provide for our family. In 2004 my business expanded when I purchased a rental unit. Working with real estate agents has worked well over the years, and with their advice, I obtained an SBA loan. This 15-year loan was paid off a few years ago. We were off and running with a moderate clean-out and mid-size rehab. After several tenants came and went, I refinanced to upgrade things, including the kitchen and windows.

The business has continued to evolve, and now we offer the Path To Home Ownership®. An example is the property above now has a couple that is renting with an option to buy.

This began in 2015 when my son Cameron and I met Lou Brown. We really liked his program and the simple way that we could help others. We both went through his whole program and became CAHP (Certified Affordable Housing Provider®) certified.

Since meeting Amy in 2017, my life and business have gotten much better.

Amy: When I got my first deal in 2018, I was hooked on real estate after that because I got a nice price that allowed me to supplement my income and help my family.

It was a duplex in a local community near us where a sister-in-law was the executrix of the estate, and she wanted nothing to do with it. The lady who owned the duplex was an "aggressive collector of books." There were 5,000 books in just one side of the duplex. I know that is a true statement because I counted them as I went through each one of them! The other side of the duplex hadn't been lived in for 30 years. When we went to look at it, I kept telling Kevin, "We're not buying this house, we're not buying this house."

I just wanted to connect with the attorney because she found our name through a probate attorney mailing, and the attorney gave her our name. The whole time, she just kept saying, "I don't know what I'm going to do with all this stuff in here." And believe me, the property was loaded with stuff. After we looked at it, I asked her what she wanted for it. She said $3,000. I said, "Okay, let me go home and "run the numbers." I had absolutely no intention of buying this house whatsoever. She called me on Monday while I was at work and said that her attorney told her she was asking too much for the property. I said, "What do you think you should get?" "Well, I think he said he wants me to get at least $1,500." Now my ears perked up. So I said, alright, let me give Kevin a call. With his advice, we offered $1,500 and split the closing costs. She agreed.

This place needed a complete rehab on both sides. One of our private lenders funded the rehab. Luckily, Kevin is a handyman, so he was able to do a lot of the work.

We put in new windows, a furnace, a kitchen, vinyl plank floors, and painted everything. We now have it rented to Path To Home Ownership® clients that we are guiding and supporting on their journey.

Our private lender is receiving regular income, and we are doing the management. This allows us to supplement our income to support our families and growth.

One of our clients had some troubles with the law in the past. As we were signing the agreement, he kept saying, "I just need somebody to give me a chance. I just really need somebody to give me a chance."

Well, now he is on the PTHO with a lease with option to buy the whole building. And he has been one of the best residents we've ever had.

Another example was again through a probate. The gentleman called us, and he was asking half of what the house was worth. And I thought, oh no, it's going to be another major cleanup or another total rehab. All right, whatever. We went to look at it, and it didn't need an ounce of work. Nothing.

I asked, "Why are you getting rid of this?" He said, "My wife had it for extra income. Since she passed, I decided to move to California to be with my daughter, and I just want to get a quick sale of it." I had a good relationship with him, and I said, "Hey, if I pay you cash for this house, will you give me a discount?" He looked at me and said, "For you? Yes."

We ended up getting a good deal, and once again, it allows us to offer affordable housing. Once again, we were able to serve a lender as we bought with borrowed money. This time it was a friend who loaned from his IRA.

So this was a win, win, win. Quick sale for the seller, safe market rate return for our lender, and a great opportunity for homeownership for our buyer!

We love this process and are looking to continue to grow and expand what we are doing for the community.

When I first met Kevin, he had the big old patchwork quilt of systems, and it wasn't working in his favor. We agreed that Lou Brown had the easiest system to follow. We've never turned back and became Platinum members in 2022. Ever since then, our business has been picking up at a fast pace.

We have such a great network of people and resources to help us. Case in point: Recently, a code officer came to do an occupancy inspection on one of our homes. He wasn't in there five minutes before he said, "I don't need to look at anything more. You guys are good." We started talking with him about the area, and I set up an afternoon where he took me out to look at vacant houses. As a result, we have about 15 properties that we're working on now to add to our portfolio.

In order to expand, we welcome new private lenders that want to earn market rates on their idle funds.

We've also become Senior Transition Specialists with Mom's House. This has opened the door to families who, for example, have a parent who might have taken a fall, is in the hospital, then on to a nursing home or a child's home because they cannot live alone anymore. So, we'll come in and purchase the home "as is," clean it out, fix it up, then rent or sell it. This way, the family doesn't have to deal with it.

Amy's background of being an Occupational Therapy Assistant who worked with seniors in their homes had many interactions with the families. Sometimes she would have to have a conversation with the family regarding her concerns about their loved one being home alone. Most times, the family would be concerned about how they would pay for the care. Now, our program can help the family get the money required for their loved one's care much quicker. We can work hand in hand with the family through this challenging transition.

As Certified Affordable Housing Providers®, we put a deserving family into the house to give them the American dream of home ownership. Without our program, many people may not have this opportunity.

In addition, Kevin has a heart for the Veterans, so he really wants to expand to providing housing for Veterans. There is a big problem with so many veterans being homeless. These brave men and women gave of themselves freely and willingly to fight for our freedom. Many even paid the ultimate price. Some returned home disabled. Providing a home for a safe place to live is Kevin's way of giving back to these brave men and women.

Amy has a heart for not only seniors but also domestic abuse victims; she would like to be able to provide shelter for them to help get them back on their feet. She is a domestic abuse survivor and has been in the position of thinking she could not get out of that situation because she didn't have anywhere to go. Being able to provide a home and a second chance for someone to start over fills her heart with joy.

Because of Lou Brown's program, Amy was able to quit the W-2 job, work in real estate full-time, and now she has the resources and knowledge to make all this happen.

About Kevin Margo and Amy Selmek

Kevin Margo and **Amy Selmek** are Certified Affordable Housing Providers® that help families to own homes regardless of credit or financial background. They have been providing homes for people for a combined 15 years and absolutely love the idea of giving the "American Dream of home ownership" to many well-deserving families!

Kevin and Amy are currently investing in the greater Pittsburgh area of Pennsylvania. Their primary investment strategy is single-family homes. They also work with private funders that use their IRAs and savings accounts to invest with them. The benefits of working with Amy and Kevin as private funders include having a sound investment using real estate and increased monthly income.

Kevin started his career as a graphic artist and, after 25 years, decided that it was time for a change. He has an entrepreneurial mindset and started a handyman business. He is experienced at repairing most aspects of the interior of a house. Working on these homes brought much satisfaction. He continues to increase his knowledge regarding buy and hold and the creative financing that goes along with it.

Doing Good While Doing Well

Starting over 15 years ago, Kevin has really enjoyed purchasing homes and offering win-win-win solutions for sellers, lenders, and buyers.

He especially enjoys providing houses to deserving families who would not otherwise be able to have the "American Dream" of owning their own homes.

Amy has a background of working closely with seniors. She's worked in the home care occupational therapy world with seniors for 13 years. Now as a Senior Transition Specialist, she assists seniors and their families in other ways, including helping families left with the decision of selling "mom's forever home" and what to do with all of the "stuff" in it. Amy purchases the home and deals with all the stuff that mom has collected over the years. She eliminates the need for a realtor and the expense and delay of "rehabbing" the home while quickly getting the money to the families so that they can get the care that mom needs in the senior care community.

She then works with a well-deserving family who wants the dream of owning their own home by using the Path To Home Ownership© program that she and Kevin offer. The new family will love the home and raise their family in it just like mom did.

Second chances have benefited them greatly, and they look forward to being of service to you whether you need a first chance or a good second chance.

To learn more about how Kevin and Amy can help you, check out their information at **www.ComfyHomes4u.com** or call **412-499-3288** or email at **CKMargo@ComfyHomes4u.com**.

"*Real estate is the key cost of physical retailers. That's why there's the old saw: location, location, location.*"

`Jeff Bezos`

Chapter 3

Dream It. Believe It. Achieve It.

Michael Thomas and Sharonda Hood

"Help others achieve their dreams, and you will achieve yours. "
~ Les Brown~

Michael and Sharonda met in college and kept in touch throughout the years. While living in California, Michael studied real estate and has a broad background, including the mortgage and insurance business, while working full-time.

Sharonda was living in Tennessee, working a full-time job as well. After years of trying to convince Sharonda to invest in real estate, she finally conceded. She admits it was not her first choice of entrepreneurship. Sharonda said, "I told Michael he had to move to Memphis if he wanted to do this real estate thing, as I was not going to do it by myself." Michael moved to Memphis and kicked off the enterprise, starting with a property-buying bus tour. The first two properties were turnkey from a company. Learning while doing and purchasing additional properties, it was like, Okay, we know how to do this now. This was when KinShip Properties, LLC was created in February 2009.

Our company has expanded its reach as we've become Certified Affordable Housing Providers®. We now offer the Path To Home Ownership® to our clients, buying and placing deserving families in homes. Michael searches for the properties, rehabs them, and offers them to our members. Ever since, we've done our due diligence and have been buying up properties. We're excited that we are helping almost 30 families now and planning for many more.

Now that we have acquired several properties in our portfolio and have met Lou Brown along our journey, Sharonda wanted to help families own their own homes. The goal is to place the current houses on the Path To Home Ownership© Program for individuals who want to buy a home and continue to buy more properties for new clients as well.

We've been able to acquire these properties in many ways, including buying subject-to (taking over existing financing), private money, hard money, owner financing, and bank financing. We particularly love using private money because it helps folks that want a safe place to put their money to work while helping us help buyers obtain home ownership.

Once we have a potential buyer, we go about finding a property for them and are open to any area they want to live in.

Even though Michael is a licensed contractor, we often help the local economy by hiring local sub-contractors. We have a lot of tools in our toolbox, so it really doesn't matter the condition of the property that we get because if we decide not to keep the property , but we feel it's still a good deal, we can outsource it to one of our many contacts in the business. But in reality, anything short of a complete gut job will work for us.

We are experienced in buying portfolios, packages of 10 and up, and single-family homes and are always open to finding homes and apartments for our future buyers.

We also have a Property Preservation division where we work with bank foreclosures and get them ready for the banks to resell them.

We love entrepreneurs and are working on a joint venture with a former tenant, who is now a business associate of ours. We purchased a dump trailer that we use for the Property Preservation. He's also a contractor with a great crew. He does a lot of renovations for out-of-state investors. So, it's an ideal situation for both of us.

Doing Good While Doing Well

Client Appreciation

When asked why are you doing this, Sharonda replied, "We had been in the business for three years and had completed our third rehab. I was buying real estate for passive income because I knew what it could provide for MY future. I presented the house to the "Johnson" family. As soon as I opened the door, "Jackson," one of the children, looked and said, "Wow! This is ours!" Jackson ran upstairs and exclaimed, "I can have my own bedroom!" The excitement he exuded touched my heart. I stood motionless and could not say anything. I snapped out of it a few seconds later to respond in small laughter with the parents. I interacted with Jackson and started explaining how the room could be decorated. As I locked up the house and drove home, I thought to myself, we work so hard for ourselves and forget about what is truly important and where we came from. Jackson, a child, told me through his behavior and excitement what I am called to do... "This is what I am supposed to do. This is helping your community with quality and affordable housing. It is not about ME anymore." I have a soft spot for kids. We rented the house to the family, and they stayed in the home for three years.

Another client, "Joe," was an older gentleman who had health issues. He had taken a 2nd mortgage out on his home to take care of necessary expenses a few years prior. He could no longer take care of his home and keep up with the mortgage payments. Joe eventually had to move in with his daughter because of health reasons. Michael met Joe through a mutual friend. We were able to help Joe by purchasing his house creatively, and we currently have the house set with a buyer on the Path To Home Ownership© program," said Sharonda

We are blessed to have many success stories - both buying and selling - with our clients and hope to help as many as possible, whether it is selling their homes or putting them in a home for the very first time.

Doing Good While Doing Well

We take our business seriously. We know that buying a home, whether it's the first or third, is daunting. When we found Lou Brown's Path To Home Ownership© Program, we knew this was right up our alley. Being a Certified Affordable Housing Provider® is how we can help families become future homeowners and is the perfect way for us to be of service.

Our mission statement is "We transform lives through affordable housing to empower families and individuals to enjoy the American dream of homeownership."

Every day in every way, we seek to be of service to our sellers, buyers, and lenders.

About Michael Thomas

Michael Thomas grew up on a one-hundred-acre farm in Northeastern Arkansas and is no stranger to hard work. He loved school, and anything associated with math would get his full attention. He majored in Electrical Engineering, got his insurance license, joined the Marine Corps, and later participated in Active Duty during Desert Storm. Being in the Marine Corps for 16+ years taught him the true meaning of discipline. He was a Team Leader of 144 Marines, and keeping them in line has given him the leadership skills to be successful in his current business. With that said, it was not difficult for him to step out on faith and start his own business.

After Michael left the Marine Corps, he worked as a network engineer for the Coast Guard in the San Francisco Bay Area. Over the next five years, he changed jobs three times, even becoming a mortgage loan originator and working in the insurance arena.

In 2008, when the financial crisis happened, he had to reinvent himself, and working for others was not the best choice for him. So, he moved to Memphis, TN, where his college girlfriend lived, and they started investing in real estate together. Michael knew real estate was the vehicle for him to start over, and at the same time, with his background and strategic planning, he knew he could help others solve their problems.

About Sharonda Hood

Sharonda Hood grew up in Central Arkansas with a family that valued education. As the saying goes, "Make good grades, get a good job, and retire, and you will be okay." Sharonda graduated with a degree in Computer Systems Engineering and a few years later received her MBA in Information Technology. She worked in corporate America for 27+ years as an Applications Developer and enjoyed life.

Although Sharonda did community service projects with organizations such as Habitat for Humanity and MIFA Meals on Wheels, and others, she wanted to do something different that would impact her community. She and Michael had several conversations while expressing that she needed to get out of her comfort zone. Things started to change around her. She saw colleagues that she worked closely with, as well as her sister, lose their jobs after 35+ years. Sharonda knew this could have been her, and she was not ready to start over. At that moment, she decided to change her way of thinking and started working with Michael to build their company, KinShip Properties, LLC, and have control of her future. Although real estate was not on her radar to make an impact, volunteering for Habitat for Humanity sparked her interest to consider it as a long-term community contribution.

Sharonda shares what she has learned as well as her experiences with anyone who cares to listen, including her sorority, Delta Sigma Theta, Inc., her car club, Strictly Vettes of Memphis/Queen Riders, her fellow colleagues at eXp Realty where she is a licensed Broker, and of course family and friends. In addition to spreading the knowledge when she can, Sharonda heads up the Property Management division of KinShip Properties, LLC.

Michael and Sharonda guide homeowners through the process of getting services set up:

(sharondahood.acnibo.com/us-en/homepage).

If clients need credit assistance to purchase a home, need a CPA, or partake in financial education, they have partnered with a company to help them through the process:

(www.mwrfinancial.com/?member=kinshipsolutionstrust).

Kinship Properties wants to be a part of helping families grow, become proud homeowners, and be a part of the solution. To learn more about how Michael and Sharonda can help you, visit or call:

KinshipPropertiesSolutions.com

MomsHouse.com

sharondahood.acnibo.com/us-en/homepage

https://www.mwrfinancial.com/membership/?member=

kinshipsolutionstrust

901-441-5516

901-443-4663

888-209-4714

Rebuilding neighborhoods… one home at a time.

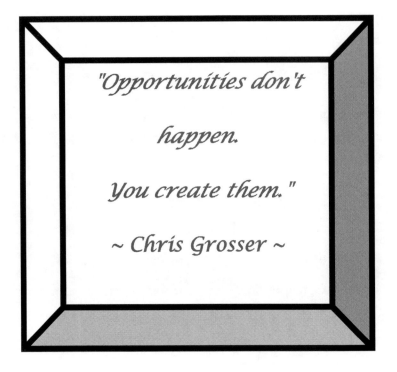

"Opportunities don't

happen.

You create them."

~ Chris Grosser ~

Chapter 4

From Renter to Investor

Kay Peck, PhD

"When the Student is Ready, the Teacher will Appear."
~Buddha~

I was born and raised in El Paso, Texas, on the border. Living so close to the border, it was a necessity to be bi-lingual, which I am. I went to school at Trinity University in San Antonio, Texas, where I received a degree in Business and Finance and a Master's degree in Healthcare Administration. I later went to the University of Texas School of Public Health and obtained my Ph.D. I currently live in San Antonio, Texas. I was a hospital CEO for 27 years until I retired.

I have an adopted daughter, and I am raising two of her children. I quickly realized that my retirement wasn't going to allow me to lead the lifestyle I wanted for the kids or me. So, after retirement, I worked hard and got my real estate license.

I didn't look into real estate blindly. My background as a consultant and later as a turnaround specialist allowed me to work in development, construction, design, layout, and flow. I opened seven new hospitals and finished the construction, and renovated and expanded seven others. The last one I worked on was a completely new build. I worked with the contractors and regulatory bodies in California, hired all the staff, recruited the medical staff, and opened it on time and under budget. Before that, I finished construction on a transformed hospital, renovated another, put together new programs, added to the bottom line, and then expanded them. I learned how to negotiate with contractors on big-ticket rehabs and purchases, which gave me a leg-up when I started doing my own personal purchases and rehabs. I knew how to deal with the permitting process on a much grander scale. I had a very well-rounded experience, which I felt would translate well into real estate.

After I got my license, I thought I was going to be very innovative in the real estate world. I joined a group of other hospital CEOs who convinced me that I should do luxury, so my sphere of influence would feed me. After nine months of doing that virtually, I got very frustrated. It just wasn't working for me, so I went to work for Keller Williams. I got good training with them and closed a few deals under each broker. However, when I had trouble getting paid, they decided to move locations, and the whole KW office was in chaos. I knew I needed a change, and luckily, I was recruited by Watters International. They provided all the leads, and I thought that this was a great way to get some real actual listing experience. In three months, I got 12 listing contracts and closed three in 90 days. Then I got my first paycheck. I couldn't believe that out of the $24,000 in commissions on my deals, I walked away with $4,100. This wasn't going to work. Once again, I moved on and joined ExP.

Working at ExP has proven to be the right move. They are very caring and patient. I didn't grow up with the type of technology that we have today. They helped me learn social media, taught me about landing pages and squeeze pages, and how to do Facebook advertising and everything that goes along with it. It was a big learning curve for me, but I've gotten over my fears and know I can master technology even when it doesn't work! I was introduced to Gary Wilson's Global Investor Agent group, and I felt at home with the people, the can-do attitude and the collegiality. Gary introduced me to Lou Brown, and Lou Brown got me into the Path To Homeownership©. I feel like the program is something I can do, something I can believe in, and I'm very excited about being a part of helping people achieve their dream of home ownership.

Over the years, I've renovated three properties that I've kept as rentals so that I have that extra income coming in. One was a home that I bought in an auction and lived in for three years. When I moved back to San Antonio, I rented it out. I had it rented for almost eight years with different renters when the last renter approached me about buying the home. We did some creative financing to get that house sold. Even though he was short on the money, I said OKAY, let's go ahead and close as long as I can pay off my bank mortgage, and I'll owner finance the balance of $100,000. Within a few months, I was paid in full. That was a really good deal because I bought the property for $225,000, and I sold it for $365,000.

With my next house, it came at a time when I was tired of paying the IRS. I would get a bonus, and I had to pay $20,000 to $25,000 of my bonus to the IRS. I was sick and tired of doing that and knew there had to be a better way to get tax breaks. So I told my neighbor, who was a realtor, that I was looking for something in our neighborhood that I could buy and use as a rental. She called me up and said she had a house. It was deemed to be uninhabitable because it was flooded, and all the sheetrock was cut out from the floor to a foot above. We bought it for $125,000, renovated it, and rented it out for three years. I was doing a lot of traveling with my previous job, and my husband got tired of being the landlord. We got an offer and we ended up selling it for $315,000. Another nice profit!

The next house was a money pit. After I retired, I used hard money financing through the credit union. I bought it for $275,000. I ended up putting more into it than I expected due to a broken pipe under the slab. We added on square footage, redid the carport, rewired the whole house, took it down to the studs, redid the kitchen and two bathrooms, etc. All total, I probably put in around $100,000 in much-needed repairs and renovations. I tried to sell it for what I wanted, but I couldn't get my price. So I decided, it's a great house, I'll put it up for rent. I rented it for about a year and 13 months. I ended up selling it a year later for

$450,000. I gave $5,000 in concessions, so I got $445,000. Another nice profit!

I love doing real estate, and I'm still learning. If I can make a margin, I can put up with a lot. If I can buy right and sell right, I'm interested. However, I do have specific criteria. I really don't want to deal with buyers for anything less than $300,000 - $350,000. I'll list almost anything if I think I can find a buyer, which I always do!

I was doing rentals to get experience and happened to talk to a maintenance man at an apartment I was showing. He worked at a local hospital, so we connected. He said the owner of the apartment needed help, and we connected. I now have an investor client who has 100 apartment units, several homes, 140 acres in Louisiana, and another 2,500 acres of land to sell. The apartments are older and in need of renovation and updating. She's in a partnership that is ready to dissolve and wants to sell off everything she owns and retire when the partnership dissolves. I agreed to help her keep the apartments rented while she prepared them for sale and listed with me.

Being in a national organization with Gary and Lou frees me up geographically so that I can help people pretty much anywhere. I can help my investor list a property anywhere in Texas, Louisiana, or California. Anywhere in the world!

I recently got a call from a friend who lives in California who's looking to move to Houston. She's got $20,000 saved, and she's paying $1,900 in rent. She wants to get into a home in Sugar Land, where I used to live, so I know the real estate in that area quite well.

I have another lady who was looking for her mother and her sister. They are renting a house, and the landlord is selling their home. She has

Doing Good While Doing Well

$5,000 to work with and can pay up to $1,200 a month. It's a viable lead, and I am working with her on the Path to Home Ownership© program.

We also have a property up in Hunt, Texas, which is near all the very exclusive camps in the hill country in Texas. We've got three acres and a 1,700 square foot, two-bedroom, two-bath cabin. We've leased that cabin out for several years, and I just recently completely renovated it, bringing it up to date. I put it on Airbnb, had several short-term rentals immediately, and then rented it for five months with an option to renew if I cannot find them a house to buy in that area!

I'm more aware of the opportunities available in real estate than I was before I joined the Global Investor Agent team and met Lou Brown with Street Smart Investors, and I'm excited. I'm looking to buy a new property, if not every month, then every other month. I want to supplement and build my IRA so I can live the lifestyle I want to live, as well as provide a better future for my grandchildren. I think I can work at least another eight to 10 years till I'm 80, while enjoying life in between.

About Kay Peck, PhD

Kay Peck was born and raised in El Paso, Texas, on the border. Living so close to the border, it was a necessity to be bi-lingual, which she is. Her father was an automobile mechanic and owned his own business. Her mother was a teacher and reading specialist. She grew up working from the age of 16 and got her education from Trinity University in San Antonio, Texas, where she received a degree in Business and Finance and a Master's degree in Healthcare Administration. She later went to the University of Texas School of Public Health and obtained her PhD. She currently lives and works in San Antonio, Texas.

Kay was a hospital CEO for 27 years, working with numerous Fortune 500 companies and several non-profits until she retired. Kay served on many Boards and State Associations as President, was Vice President of the San Antonio Chamber of Commerce under Mayor Nelson Wolf, served on local and statewide blue-ribbon committees, was on the Board of the Texas Hospital Association and the American Hospital Association Policy Board for many years.

Doing Good While Doing Well

Kay is a Global Investor Agent, a Certified Affordable Housing Provider, a Trust Specialist, a Certified Express Offers Agent, a Listing Specialist, a Credit Repair Agent, and a Senior Transition Specialist.

Contact information

Email - kay.peck@exprealty.com

Phone - 210-381-4010

Office - 210-953-1359

Toll Free – 833-807-3376

Fax - 977-201-4751

https://www.facebook.com/DrKaytheRealtor

https://www.instagram.com/kaypeckphd/

https://www.linkedin.com/in/kay-peck-phd-b3a40b186/

At Kay@Affordable-homesforsale.com - the Path to Home Ownership©

and at Kay@Sellingsolutionsusa.com - the Path to Home Ownership©

Doing Good While Doing Well

Chapter 5

The Song of the Entrepreneur

David Kahl

*"Our only limitation, within reason, lies in the development
and use of our imagination."*
~ Napoleon Hill~

There is a song in each one of us that, if heard and sung, will bring things into harmony in our lives and fill our days with purpose and passion. Sometimes because of the noise of life, we don't hear our song for a while, but it's there.

In 2005, while working in my first career of insurance, I was introduced to several books that were life-changing, one being *Rich Dad Poor Dad* by Robert Kiyosaki. The seed of real estate investing was planted in me but didn't take root for about ten years. I tried to apply the principles of entrepreneurship I was learning from these books to my insurance career, but things just didn't click: number one, I was doing something I liked but didn't love, and number two, I was working under the umbrella of a larger company that didn't allow me to duplicate and expand as I wanted.

At the time, it was hard to understand what was missing. I was earning a solid income, going on company trips, and living a good life, but something was just not quite in rhythm and harmony with my true desires. Then in 2015, when one of the health insurance companies drastically reduced commissions on policies I had already sold, I realized I had to make a change. Real estate had always been in the back of my mind, so after going to a seminar by T. Harv Eker in 2015, I decided to take a course in real estate. I was fascinated by it and would get up before dawn to study and make plans. In 2016, I bought my first rental property and did seven deals that year.

I knew I was on the right track but knew there was more. Sometime towards the end of 2016, I thought maybe I could put tenants in my property that could work towards purchasing the home. They would be A-class tenants because they had an interest in buying the home and would take care of it. At the time, I didn't know anything about lease options or rent-to-own. One day while journaling, an idea struck me like a bolt of lightning. What if I could purchase properties with owner financing at a discounted price and then turn around and sell them for a higher price with owner financing and create cash flow for myself while providing a solution for the seller as well as homeownership for the new buyer? It would be a win-win-win. I remember that moment distinctively: I jumped out of my chair and started acting like a football player that just scored the winning touchdown in the Super Bowl. I had found my song, and I still know it's my song because as I write on this beautiful morning, I'm sitting on the porch of the Grand Bohemian Lodge, having to hold back tears of passion since I am in public. I thought it might be odd if people see me sitting over here by myself, crying as I type.

The idea for this business came from personal experience. I had struggled as a young entrepreneur in my 20s without a mentor to guide me, but I held on to a quote I heard that my biggest weaknesses could become my biggest strengths. At the time, my wife, three kids, and I lived in an apartment while making a six-figure income because we didn't know how to buy a home because traditional bank financing doesn't like the self-employed. Now, not only do we own a beautiful home, but we help many others own their own home for the first time through lease options and owner-financing. The struggle we once had with borrowing money and banks running from us has turned into a business in which millions of dollars from investors have poured into and have paid back solid returns.

Napoleon Hill wrote in *Think and Grow Rich*, "Our minds become magnetized with the dominating thoughts we hold in our minds, and these magnets attract to us the forces, the people, the circumstances of life which harmonize with the nature of our dominating thoughts."

In 2017, my song, my dominating thought was to create a business model in which we would help others have the dream of home ownership, but I didn't know how to make it happen. It was simply a pulsating desire. Shortly after, I met one of Lou Brown's students and heard about the "Path to Home Ownership©" program Lou had developed. I became a student of Lou, and everything started coming together. Everything started to harmonize, and business started booming. My original plan was to build a portfolio of rentals and, after 10-15 years, have enough passive income from real estate to leave my insurance career. But once I started applying the Path to Home Ownership and learned the power of lease options and owner-financing, a year-and-a-half later I was making more part-time in real estate than in my full-time career. My 10-15 year plan was accelerated to 1 ½ years! Business was taking off while others were winning with a good return on investments and families with home ownership. What a fantastic business model!

Currently, we are acquiring 2-4 homes a month, and this is our best year yet. We have a 21-home packet under contract now and are partnering with Lou Brown on this deal. And all this is being done without the banks and big financial institutions. Private individuals are funding all of these deals as well as us purchasing through owner-financing and subject-to.

We are looking for individuals that would like to put their money to work in this business to get a good return while holding their money in asset-based real estate, providing a secure investment. We are looking for individuals who would also like to "Do Good while Doing Well." This model can give yields much better than most investments. It almost makes me cry when I see someone with an IRA that's getting 1-2% just so they can stay in a safe investment. They don't want to "lose" money, but they are losing big to inflation.

Some take more risks to get a higher return in the stock market, but because it is not asset-based, like real estate is, they take a beating in certain markets. Like one of my investors said, "I made $20,000 in the stock market in the past year! But I also lost $25,000." Why not invest in something that gives solid returns, is backed by real estate assets, and at the same time serves a good cause by helping families and individuals achieve the dream of home ownership?

Andrew Carnegie was the wealthiest man in America in the early 1900s. He made the following statement: "90% of millionaires become so through owning real estate. More money has been made than in all the industrial investments combined. The wise young man or wage earner of today invests his money in real estate." This still holds true today. Real estate, if done correctly, is a powerful tool to build wealth safely.

Purpose-Driven

The fuel for our business is purpose and passion versus simply financial freedom. I want to always be financially free, and I love traveling, fine dining, and nice things, but this is not the destination. I absolutely want the best for my wife and four kids, but the best is not just financial security - it's building a family legacy! Everywhere you look on social media, you see gurus promoting building a business so you never have to work again, or you can have a 4-hour work week. There is absolutely nothing wrong with that, but we want to make a positive impact in this world, impact lives, and build something that lives beyond ourselves.

Doing Good While Doing Well

This business of helping others have solid returns by investing in real estate while helping families and individuals own their first home goes beyond ourselves to change lives.

Recently I had a friend ask me, "David, you have a large portfolio; you've already accomplished a lot. Why are you still working? You need to slow down and ask yourself why you are working so hard." I get what he was saying, but he missed the point. If you are strictly thinking about growing the business so "you" can have more things, more free time, and more money in the bank, sure, I understand why you would would "retire young" rather than just focus on stacking up the bank account. But what about all the good you can do for others with your business and wealth? And what if your business is your hobby, and if you love what you do - then it is not work. That's why I don't feel I'm working hard because I love what I do. Every day is a vacation. This is my sport, and yes, I do things I don't want to do, just as an athlete pushes his/her muscles to pain, but it's what I'm passionate about. Our purpose is our life book, and we are writing it each day. Why not make it a great story?

I believe in family, and this is a family business. My wife and I work together and involve the kids, and we have a freakin' blast. It's changed our lives, developed us into leaders, and we find joy in what we do as we do it together.

We want to grow and lead a team of people that will create an investment business, not just be an individual investor. Robert Kiyosaki, in his book "Cash Flow Quadrant," talks about the difference between a self-employed person versus a true business owner. The self-employed person is the business, drives the business, does the job of the technician, etc., while the business owner creates systems and leads teams, and the business takes on a life of its own.

Doing Good While Doing Well

As stated earlier, we are currently purchasing 2-4 properties a month, but our current goal is to acquire 100 properties a year in our local market. Once we accomplish this, we would like to take this model to other markets, as well as develop other entrepreneurs. As Lou Brown says, "The goal of CAHP is to change housing in America for the better," and I want to be a big part of this.

Many times when our home buyers move up the Path to Home Ownership from the Lease Option level to the Owner-Financed level, we go visit the home. It's a beautiful thing to walk into a family's home, a home that was once vacant and plain and now full of life. Freshly baked food, new paint, and upgrades they are proud to have done on their home, pictures on the walls of family memories, a garden planted on the land they now own, a handshake with a big smile and a thank you. These are the things we experience that are so rewarding. All while, at the same time, we are helping investors get a solid and secure return where they once were getting 1-2% in the bank or exposed to the volatility of the market. And we are helping to improve neighborhoods, cities, local governments, etc. It's a WIN, WIN, WIN! To me, this is the true meaning of "Doing Good While Doing Well."

About David Kahl

The formation of **David Kahl's** business was built out of passion and personal experience. As a young entrepreneur with no mentorship, he met many hardships in his twenties. He had a very difficult time finding traditional bank financing to buy his first home, and at one point, he, his wife, and three kids were living in a small apartment. But he held onto the hope from something he read that his biggest weaknesses would be his biggest strengths.

Through perseverance and reading book after book on self-development and entrepreneurship, the principles of success began to take root in David's life. He bought his first home off market with over $100,000 in equity. Bells went off in him on the power of real estate that he had read about from authors like Robert Kiyosaki and Robert Allen. After investing for a year, he found what he calls his "Song," his passion that turned his work and business into a musical harmony that began to flow like a musician creating a song. His struggle to own his own home gave him the idea of helping others obtain homeownership through owner-financing his real estate deals to individuals and families, and from his difficulty with money earlier in his career was born the passion for helping others invest passively in real estate in his deals. At last, he turned his greatest weaknesses into his greatest strengths.

When David met Lou Brown in 2017, his "Song" was able to become a reality as he learned the ins and outs of how to use lease options and owner financing through Lou's Path to Home Ownership© program. Currently, David is acquiring 2-4 homes a month and is using private financing from individuals to fund his deals while giving them a good return on their investment. Individuals and families are owning their homes for the first time because of his efforts. The financial success his family is now reaping, combined with doing something he loves by helping others with home ownership and good returns on investment, for David, is the meaning of "Doing Good while Doing Well."

If you would like to find out more about how to invest with David's company for solid returns and to be part of their mission of providing home ownership, feel free to call David at **828-458-5610** or visit his website at **carolinafirsthome.com.**

Chapter 6

Son of An Immigrant, Living The American Dream

Harry St. Louis

"Do good, and good will come to you."

On this wonderful journey called life, there are many stops along the way; each stop presents a set of opportunities. Opportunity is defined as a set of circumstances that makes it possible to accomplish something. Therefore, it is imperative that one executes on the set of circumstances and accomplishes something; otherwise, you lose that opportunity. Over time, opportunities executed really define who we become and the level of success that we achieve.

My parents moved to New York from Haiti when I was nine years old, which created a wealth of opportunities for my three sisters and for me. My mom worked two jobs to be able to support us and put us through college. We lived in a one-bedroom apartment for about two years before we could afford to rent a three-bedroom apartment. Drive, passion, and motivation are the values that I inherited from mom as I acknowledge how hard she worked to provide for us and position us to succeed. To that end, my sisters and I are all college graduates. I've earned a bachelor's and two master's degrees in Management Information Systems and Project Management. Along the way, my sisters and I got to enjoy the American dream of homeownership as we all have a primary residence that we own and, for me, investment properties as well.

My real estate journey started in 2001 when my wife and I bought our first house in New York. We then set our sights on purchasing a few more properties. However, things didn't really kick into gear until we moved to Georgia in 2004. My wife and I bought our first property in Georgia with cash in 2005. We fixed it up, lived in it for a year, moved out, rented it, and bought another house. We fixed up our next house and had every intention of renting it until my wife turned it into a personal care home. We stumbled onto another exit strategy. However, we made lots of costly mistakes along the way. Nevertheless, we continued with the real estate buy-and-hold strategy. In 2012 I expanded into a full-service real estate company: wholesale, buy and hold, and fix and flips.

The expansion into a full-service real-estate company was trial by fire. Without a proven, well-defined model, I made a lot of mistakes and lost some money. Fortunately, I met and joined Lou Brown's group in 2016, and he became my mentor. I earned the *Certified Affordable Housing Provider*® (CAHP) designation. This was the best move I ever made in my quest to grow my real estate business. From that point on, I was able to avoid the pitfalls inherent in real estate investing because of Lou's mentoring.

I love the *Path To Homeownership*® Program. I was blessed to be able to live the American Dream of Homeownership and understand the difference it makes in the quality of life personally and financially. Therefore, the PTHO Programs resonated with me profoundly. We love the fact that we are able to work with clients to provide that dream and, at the same time, build a portfolio of properties. I remember helping a newly divorced mom who lost her home to foreclosure. She and her seven-year-old daughter were suddenly without a home. I was able to leverage the *Path To Homeownership*® Program to help her move into a home that I owner financed for her. Within a three-year period, with the credit repair service that we provide as part of the PTHO program, she was able to obtain an FHA Loan to cash me out and obtain a mortgage in her name. This is the type of result that makes the program gratifying. She was able to move into a home, not an apartment, with her daughter; eventually, she was able to outright purchase the home. For me, I was able to help this family while making a living. To quote the title of this book, "Doing Well While Doing Good," it is a wonderful Win/Win Situation.

I've continued to leverage the many strategies that I learned as part of Lou's mentorship. A simple script I learned from Lou helped me to develop a private lender relationship with individuals that I would never think would lend me money to purchase homes. Lou's mentorship has helped me to make money but, even more importantly, has kept me from losing money. I remember reaching out to Lou for feedback on a property that I was planning on rehabbing and flipping. I had grand plans to convert this 900 sq. ft. 2-bedroom 1-bath house into a 3000 sq. ft. 4-bedroom 3-bath renovated home. After Lou had me go through the Property Acquisition Worksheet and reviewed it with me, I realized that this project was a loser. As a result, I scrapped it expeditiously and avoided a financial pitfall.

My focus at this point is buy-hold. No matter how well our business is doing, we are constantly looking for sellers, buyers, and investors. Obviously, the more sellers that we have, the more investors we need. Getting access to that private money helps tremendously. It allows us to close quickly. We currently live in Snellville, Georgia, and Gwinnett County is a hot spot for real estate. The average median listing home price is $255,000 in Snellville and $275,000 in Gwinnett County. The average median listing home price in Fulton County, which includes Atlanta, is $350,000. So, by having less expensive homes (not less valued), people are clamoring to purchase here. As the metro Atlanta area continues to grow, the opportunities are abundant.

In closing, when I first met Lou, I was at a crossroads. I knew I was doing good, but I knew I could do better. When I became a CAHP and started leveraging the *Path To Homeownership® Program*, it was the missing piece of the puzzle. My parents created opportunities for me and my siblings when they came to the United States. I feel like it is my duty to help others less fortunate. The people that we work with are good, hardworking people, but they may have had a few misfortunate missteps. They've been through a divorce, landed up homeless (while still keeping a job), had large medical bills that affected their credit score, etc. Many have families that they want to give the best to. Owning their own home means security for their family. How can I turn my back on their needs? Giving back to our community is rewarding. With this program, I am able to help our sellers, buyers, and investors. Our memberships offer lease options, work for equity programs and owner financing. We try and make it easy for our clients. It's very humbling to know you've changed someone's life for the better. The story I told earlier about the mom who lost her home to foreclosure, and I was able to get her into a home, is a classic example of making a difference in the life of others through the *Certified Affordable Housing® Program* as well as making a difference in the community. By buying vacant houses or houses that are in disarray, we help revitalize the community. When people own their own home, they are more prone to take care of it by painting, keeping the lawn mowed and clear of debris, etc. They take pride in their accomplishment. With most rentals, this is not possible, so many just give up and accept that this is how they have to live. But by having your own home, you can make all the changes you want, and nobody can tell you "No." And by having a well-kept home, this increases the value of their neighborhood.

By putting people on the *Path to Home Ownership®* Program, many times we get the full asking price for the home because comparing other home prices is not really an option that our clients typically are concerned about. We also make a difference in the seller's lives because we are ready to buy their home immediately. This gives them the opportunity to move on with their lives sooner than later. So, to end with the word that I started with, "Opportunity," that is what The *Path To Homeownership®* *Program* provides.

About Harry St. Louis

Harry St. Louis is a serial entrepreneur, having started several businesses. He is currently retired from Corporate America after a 30 plus year career in the corporate world, which included 17 years at Morgan Stanley and 14 years at Cisco Systems.

Harry is first and foremost a believer in our Lord Jesus Christ! He is a husband and a father, having married the world's greatest wife, his love, Marie. He is blessed with two daughters, Nadege and Nickille, and a granddaughter, Chassidy. He enjoys spending time with his family, worshiping, hiking, walking, music, and playing the drums. These days Harry spends his time as a core group bible study leader, cooking for his wife, day trading in the stock market, and managing his real estate business. This is Harry in a nutshell!!

Office: 678-318-7510

Cell: 770-866-6598

Harry.StLouis@RealEstate-Concepts.com

www.realestate-concepts.com

"There are two types of people who will tell you that you cannot make a difference in this world: those who are afraid to try and those who are afraid you will succeed."

~ Ray Goforth ~

Chapter 7

Everyone Has A Different Story
and A Different Situation

Tracy Mills

"Among the things you can give and still keep are your word, a smile, and a grateful heart." ~Zig Ziglar~

I grew up in a very small town of about 600 people in a rural farming community. Since there weren't a lot of opportunities other than farming, I moved away as soon as I got out of high school. Because of the downturn in agriculture, our income was reduced to almost zero, our home was in foreclosure, and my parents were forced to move to a bigger city. I ended up working for the fire department in Columbia, South Carolina, and when I turned 21, I went to work for the highway patrol here in the state of South Carolina. When I worked for the fire department, I had quite a bit of downtime. Since I had always been involved in some type of construction around our house growing up, I started working with contractors rehabbing houses. I learned how to rehab, worked with woodworking, like cabinet making, and eventually learned how to actually build houses. Around 2004 when it was time for me to own my own home, I heard about rent-to-own or lease-purchase. That got me really excited because I could do this without having a lot of money. And I could also help people that couldn't normally buy a house any other way. So, I started buying up houses really fast. I had around 60 houses when the market crashed in 2008. Had I known then what I know now, I would have walked right through that with no problem. But I saw a lot of people losing everything they had, got a bit scared, and sold everything for what I had in it and got out. I got away from real estate for a little while, just because it was so bad.

But it turned out that real estate became a passion of mine. It got a hold of me and wouldn't let go! So, I got back in and started to gravitate towards systems that would make me more successful. And of course, the Path to Homeownership® is exactly what I needed to help people that can't get help anywhere else. And I've just really grown my business from there.

A Work-for-Equity Home

A work-for-equity home is just what it sounds like. The work you do in your own home is applied to your down payment or used to lower your monthly payment. This program is an opportunity for the buyer that provides them with affordable monthly payments. They are able to buy their first home through my program, with as little as 10% down, and I help teach them how they can be successful in this endeavor.

Achieving the goal of homeownership is not easy. One must have a good credit score, adequate savings to put down as a deposit, and sufficient income to afford monthly mortgage payments. I offer buyers an affordable payment plan that is tailored to their monthly budget and financial goals, as well as being mindful of any other debt they might be carrying, such as student loans or car payments. We work with a lot of self-employed clients that have a hard time qualifying traditionally. My team and I will work closely alongside buyers and provide them with the knowledge they need to be successful homeowners.

I love helping people become homeowners through my "work-for-equity" program. I work closely alongside them throughout the process of becoming a homeowner and help teach them how to be successful in this endeavor. Knowledge is what people need to be successful homeowners, so I make sure that they understand every step on their journey with my team by providing personalized coaching and education.

Doing Good While Doing Well

I am currently working in the Lowcountry in the state of South Carolina, where prices are a bit on the high side. There are still deals here, but they're wildly expensive. Since I come from more of the rural area and am familiar more with those types of homes as well as the people, I like to venture out into those areas, where I'm finding some pretty good deals. There are a lot of people in these areas that need housing desperately. So, that's where my passion lies. I am learning to work remotely and utilize people on the ground in those areas and see if we can help more than the areas other than just where we live. The lower half of South Carolina is where I'm focusing, but I am open to finding great properties all around the whole state.

I've found in those rural areas that there are a lot of people who are qualified for our program but have been denied because their credit score is too low. They would be perfect candidates to work through our affordable housing programs. First, we can get them into their home, and then we can help them improve their credit. People get really excited about that. They are like, "Wow, this is something I could afford." So, my goal would be to find an area where there's low inventory and then go from there and see how much demand there is.

I love the Work for Equity Program the most because it solves a homebuyer's problems. Since they are doing most of the work in the home, as opposed to me doing it, they look at the home from a different point of view. They'll fix it up the way they want to fix it up. They get to do the work and are given credit towards their down-payment. It's a win-win for everyone involved. It's called Work To Own because you work for your future house. People earn their own equity in a house through the labor they put into it.

I'm working in an area right now in a community in South Carolina that has been a rental community for probably the last 30 years. It's gone really downhill, and nobody takes care of the property. I just bought a house there for $10,000, and we've placed it on our Work For Equity Program. We've also put options on other houses, and we're trying to go in and change the neighborhood one house at a time. It's my long-term goal, and if we can do it, it will change a lot of people's lives for the better and the community they live in.

More and more people are becoming homeowners, thanks to affordable homeownership options that provide those who may have been denied conventional mortgage access to the American Dream of owning their own home. More than four million Americans owe their homes to programs like these, which offer them an opportunity for stable homeownership, while also providing a return on investment for investors. And that's what keeps me in this business.

It's life-changing when you can have an effect on your community. And when you can give someone a chance to buy their first house at 45 years old or 55 years old, and they're so thankful for the opportunity, it's the best feeling in the world. Everybody needs a chance and the opportunity to own their own home. There's nothing better than that feeling of pride when you can achieve that unattainable dream for yourself and your family. It's security at its best. For me, it's invigorating, and it really makes me want to go find another house and keep doing the right thing. It's my reward at the end of the day. In addition, you're not just making a profit, you're literally changing people's lives.

So, when you are ready for your first home purchase but don't know how it's possible because of any or all these challenges, turn to me. I have a solution: my Work-For-Equity program, which enables people of all backgrounds the opportunity for homeownership.

Lenders Wanted

Our big thing right now is trying to align ourselves with private money.

Doing Good While Doing Well

We can find the deals, do the work, and make a profit, but it takes money to grow in this business. And when you can create the money flow, that helps things accelerate quickly.

At this point, I am leaning towards finding more lenders than equity partners. But I won't turn either away! I love building relationships with both. What I'm looking for is somebody that really wants to help people become homeowners and won't object to a piece of the pie.

I'm looking for somebody that has a little bit of money in CDs, Ira's, money market accounts, or even sitting in a checking or savings account and would like to make above-market rates. I want to create an environment where they don't have to work but still make a good profit on their investment.

What we're trying to do is find people who are really willing to build relationships with us and help our clients be homeowners. And I'm not a greedy person, either. I like to make my lenders want to come back. I believe 5-8 % is a reasonable price to pay for funding, and it's a wonderful return for the investors compared to what they're getting, especially when I show them how to use the money in their 401k or their IRA.

I believe we have some of the best rates in the business, and it's an investment that will outperform the stock market. I'm just looking for people that are willing to help us make other people's lives better.

About Tracy Mills

Tracy Mills grew up in a small town of 600 people and moved away after high school and worked as a Firefighter for the city of Columbia, and later became a State Trooper for the South Carolina Highway Patrol, where he served for 5 Years.

Over the years, he has worked many jobs in the construction industry, from cabinet building to whole house construction and even staircase building.

Tracy's passion is finding great deals on homes that can be fixed up and helping families get started toward owning their own homes. But he was still falling short on helping people truly end up with homeownership doing the things he had learned, so he set out to find a better way. One thing he has learned is that every house has a different story, and every buyer/seller has a different situation. So, you just have to listen and figure out the best way to help bring a solution.

Tracy has concentrated on becoming an expert in his field and continues to stay educated and unrelentingly learn from the ever-changing world of real estate.

Doing Good While Doing Well

Tracy has completed his required certification for the Certified Affordable Housing Provider® program, as well as becoming a Certified Deal Specialist, Certified Trust Specialist, Certified Income Specialist, a Master of Business Advancement, and specializing in Quiet title issues. As a member of the Platinum Mastermind group, Tracy meets with other certified affordable housing providers from all across the country every four months in order to stay right on the pulse of what is going on in the real estate business.

With this ever-changing world, it is of utmost importance to stay up to date on things going on in the real estate world. We have just gone through a never-experienced shut down of our world, and we were able to continue to serve our clients and look forward to getting back to work to help more clients as we move forward.

Tracy does a lot of networking and reaches out to county governments and programs to bring this concept to as many people as possible. It is genuinely a MISSION.

Tracy is married to his soulmate, and they have six wonderful children and two grandchildren between them. They live in Historic Charleston, SC, and enjoy everything that goes with living in the low country.

For a free no-obligation consultation, please reach out to Tracy and see how he and the Live Oak Solutions team can help you with your unique house selling and/or buying needs.

www.myliveoaksolutions.com

www.lohomebuyers.com

Tracy@myliveoaksolutions.com

843-278-1888

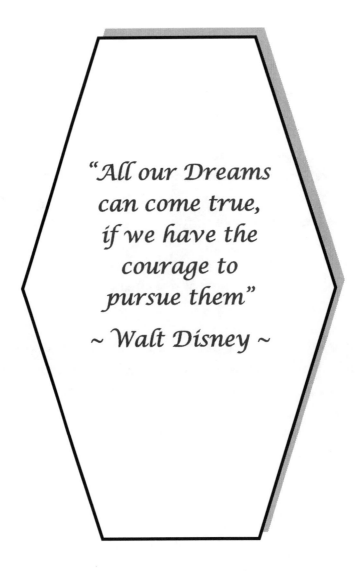

"*All our Dreams can come true, if we have the courage to pursue them*"

~ Walt Disney ~

Chapter 8

How a Tenant House Sealed My Future

John McConnell

"There are three things you can do with your life: You can waste it, you can spend it, or you can invest it. The best use of your life is to invest it in something that will last longer than your time on Earth."
~ Rick Warren~

I come from very humble beginnings. I grew up on a farm, and we were dirt poor. We lived off the land and didn't have much money at all, just for the bare necessities. When I was a kid, we had a tenant house on the farm where the hired help lived. Back then, the rent was $25 a month. Whenever we needed something, my mother would say that we couldn't buy anything until the rent came in. So whenever that $25 payment came in, we were able to buy what we needed, big or small, but most of the time, it was needed for food. I remember it was time for me to go to first grade. Unfortunately, I didn't have a good pair of shoes to wear to school, so I had to wait for the rent to come in. I eventually got a pair of shoes to wear and was so proud that I could finally go to school. That stuck with me growing up, and I vowed I would do something other than farming so that my family or I never had to go through that again.

As I got older, I realized I could make money from real estate. Maybe it was because we had the rent coming in from our tenant house. So I bought a rental home. I rented that house for a while, and then I sold it and bought another one, then another, and another. But after a while, I got tired of fighting with my tenants, so I sold them all. But, as it happens many times, I got bored and needed extra money, so I bought and sold more houses. I eventually decided to buy my own farm (I guess it's in my blood), but the bank wouldn't loan me money because they said my debt ratio was out of balance. I ended up liquidating everything at bargain-basement prices to buy my farm. Once I bought my farm, I needed extra money to fix the property, so I started buying houses again! It sounds like a vicious cycle, doesn't it? Today I have ten rental properties, and I will continue to purchase properties until I get what Lou would refer to as "20 houses free and clear" so that I can retire and still have a nice income.

I don't think I ever fully considered real estate as a means to my retirement when I first started. I guess I thought of it as an *addition* to my retirement or as an easy way to make extra money. For 30 years, I worked for a utility company until they let me go due to health problems. Unfortunately, I had to sue them for my retirement money. It's sad when you have to spend your money to get your money! But I eventually did get my retirement money and invested it with a broker who put most of the money into an annuity. When I turned 65 and wanted to draw my retirement, I was told I was better off leaving it so that it could mature a little more. After a year of fighting them for my money (once again), I now have my retirement under my control.

Being a full-time farmer as well as a full-time investor keeps me busy. I prefer to purchase single-family homes because not only are they easier to flip than multi-family units, people need a house, and for me, they are easier to buy. I have bought multi-units in the past, and I have a really good local financial resource. Anytime I needed money, they said, "how much?" But truthfully, I prefer not to deal with multi-units. Even though management companies primarily deal with the units, it's just too much of a hassle for me at this time in my life.

I love getting a good deal, and I'm always looking for bargains. I'm not tethered to my area, so if I hear of a great deal in Alaska, I'll look into it. If I can make good money but don't have to be there, I will consider the deal.

I've always been fortunate with my funding. Besides an occasional loan from my local bank, the majority of my money has come from the profits of my sales and recently from my retirement money. I don't need to rely on investors to make a deal work. I might be a rarity in that respect, but I'm very independent and have always prided myself on being a one-man show. My concern is to make my buyers happy, not investors.

I'm the type of person who is always learning, especially in this business. I love the aspect of the Certified Affordable Housing Provider® (CAHP) program as well as the Rent to Own program. I'm currently working with a gentleman named Scott Patton to help perfect my trade within these programs. He's helping me to make my business bigger and stronger. However, he does have his work cut out for him because I'm the type of person who doesn't follow orders very well. Usually, I'll take suggestions, mull them over, then do what I feel is best. It's been working for me for over 60 years, so why stop now?

People say that good professional advice is the mark of every successful person. As successful as I am, it's a rarity for me to work with professionals. However, Lou Brown is an exception to that rule. That man is smart! Many times when I've tried to work with other professionals in my field, it ended up that I actually knew more than they did because I've been in the business a lot longer than they have. I've also met many people who think that because they've read a few books, they can now call themselves a coach. Maybe I have this attitude because I've been burnt a few times in the past. However, I am smart enough to know that if I do need help with something, I will always look for the very best.

That's what I want for my clients - to work with the very best. I've been in this business all my life. I know the building aspect. I know the financial aspect. I know how to rehab. I know the best areas to buy in. I know the real estate market.

Doing Good While Doing Well

Being a Certified Affordable Housing Provider® (CAHP), I have options that others do not have. With our Rent To Own program, I can get buyers who have bad credit or little to no down payments a home that they can be proud of. Instead of putting down a huge monetary down-payment, with sweat equity we can show them how to do repairs in the home, which will go towards their down-payment. This also keeps our repair costs down. I love it when people say that they've never met anyone like us and that if it wasn't for our programs, they would never have the opportunity to own their own homes.

About John McConnell

John McConnell learned early in life that owning real estate can offer opportunities that wouldn't exist otherwise. Through his 40 plus year real estate career, he has learned the right and wrong way to do things, sometimes by doing them the wrong way first. Some might call it the "school of hard knocks." If you want to see a diploma, get ready to look at a history of scars. All this education has helped him to refine the focus areas for his operations. He has focused on single-family homes and has experience in rentals, flips and extensive rehab.

Always striving for the next opportunity with a sense of optimism that seems to be contagious with entrepreneurs, he continues to look for ways to expand his real estate business. He currently works with a team that he feels is on the same page and intends to focus purchase opportunities in upper-class areas and liquidate some properties that have been headaches. He seeks to help people in distress by solving their problems with unique solutions for owning their own homes. Focusing on what is important to him, he continues helping people and his family and maintains a continual goal of building a solid retirement and creating a business that is generational.

Doing Good While Doing Well

John resides in a rural town in Pennsylvania where he continues to operate his real estate operation in addition to farming a 120 acre farm. Pick a hot sunny summer day and you'll likely find him baling hay, another of his true passions. He has a wife (Bonnie) and two grown children. He can be reached online at **www.horizonhomesales.com** or directly via email at **McConnellFarmandHome@yahoo.com** and by phone at **724-986-2640**.

Chapter 9

Starting Out? Starting Over? Start with Shelly!

By Shelly Fonner

"What you think about and talk about, you bring about!"
"Change your thoughts – Change your life!"

I started my real estate investing career as a single Mom – wanting really hard to change where I was and where I was headed. Coming from a family of 'workers' in the same industry for 40+ years, there sure wasn't a support system backing my decision to become an entrepreneur. As I was raised by my Mom (she and Dad divorced when I was 3), I watched the many struggles my family would go through. Even though they were gainfully employed most of the year through, their wages were low and conditions painful to watch as they aged. In my young eyes, I felt they were treated unfairly, unjustly, and worked in conditions beyond what was acceptable. They were proud of their accomplishments, as it did put food on the table, but living conditions were meek, to say the least. Plus, I felt determined to change this cycle – It was up to me to be different, change things as they say... otherwise – I would fall trapped to having this same lifestyle. After all, we are what we see, right? We become our environment. That is unless we take a different, less-traveled road... in which I set out to do.

Making a decision to become a real estate investor is just the first step in making this happen. After all – not having anyone 'close' to council you, advise you, encourage you (I could go on and on), you really start from scratch, trying to figure out not only what you want to do but HOW you are going to do what you set out to do.... (the simple task of changing your life!). I chose real estate investing for two reasons really: 1) I had a huge interest in real estate – from houses, floor plans, prices, and people and 2) I had read and heard that many millionaires were created from investing in real estate. This seemed to be the perfect combo to me ☺

Setting out to figure which program, teacher, 'guru' I would follow was an overwhelming process in the beginning. I would spend hours online reading about which person offered what, which 'intro' offer was appealing, what 'bonus' sessions they were giving away, and what type of testimonials they had. Do this a few times over and I promise it all runs together.

In reading the motivational books about changing your life – creating your new-found freedom – becoming an entrepreneur – changing bad habits into lasting good habits, etc., (those of you that have attempted to totally transform your surroundings know exactly what I'm talking about), it's crucial that you read books that talk about how to do this. The last I checked, we don't come with an owner's manual on how to do a 180, so this is important in making these changes a reality versus just a conversation I had with myself. These books would talk about my thoughts, actions, perseverance, and commitment needed to go against the odds. The stories inside these pages would motivate me beyond the daily grind and give me hope that if they could do these things, then I could, too!

The good news about real estate investing is you don't have to know everything to get started, nor will you, regardless of how much reading you spend on the topic. There are so many avenues for you to explore. The important part is to find a mentor and go for it! I've always said it's an Aim, Fire, Ready (not Ready, Aim, Fire) type of situation – you can adjust as you move along! Notice I said *find a mentor* – I don't want you to skip over that part or put it on the back burner – I believe it is crucial on how quickly you will grow your business! Find a mentor and get going... you will expand, change, adapt, and explore even more once you have a foundation, but do not skip this step!

Doing Good While Doing Well

I dabbled in real estate about 10+ years ago but didn't really get off the ground much. I bought a couple of houses with owner financing and went to the bank and got a loan on a couple, and then I allowed life to get all busy. My full-time 'job' took over (I even went through a divorce – ouch!), and I had settled into the 'landlord and toilets' scenario that was not super exciting to me! You know the stories that everyone has warned you about the minute you told them you wanted to explore real estate – you will soon find that everyone has their 'horror' story about tenants. I was once told that you have headaches and moments of chaos with any J.O.B… so why not have it be your own headache and chaos and create the life you want at the same time? I realized this was a good point. During this time of struggle, I really had no guidance or mentor, as I described to you above. I was doing everything the hard way: no system, no proven agenda…just buying things the traditional way and honestly, the wrong way, but I didn't even know it. This is why I am telling you that having a Mentor and someone you can follow and get advice from is going to be crucial in how well and how quickly you build your business. (Make sure this mentor or guide to your business is successful and further along than you are!) Their experience can shave years off of your business growth, not to mention, save you thousands!

To give you an idea of how important a mentor is to your overall success, once I found a mentor and followed their system exactly as outlined, I went from buying 3-4 homes ever to closing over 20 homes PER YEAR! I promise you, a mentor who is currently involved in the real estate industry will explode your business! The only changes to what I was doing before were having a system to follow! I didn't wake up one day with ALL the answers, I didn't get a ton of cash to buy these houses (as a matter of fact, I bought all these houses with NONE of my own money), and I was still single! I even created a busier life by adopting four children from the foster program while I was a foster parent. See… we can be all kinds of busy and still find a way to change our lives, our circumstances and see our dreams unfold before us. It takes Determination, Dedication, and a Desire to make it happen! The 3 D's are what successful people talk about. If you haven't been taught these principles or maybe, like me, these things hadn't been discussed ever, then we have to educate ourselves in order to change our lives! Remember, if it were easy to change our circumstance and make our dreams come true, then every single person would be doing it! I believe it is simple (follow the system), but it's not easy.

Keeping It In The Bank

Now that I've taken some time to explain to you where I started (to show you that if I can do it, you can do it too), I would like to talk more about the above statement I made – buying 20+ properties per year and not using my money! What would you say if I said not only did I not use MY money, I didn't use ANY money!? After all – I didn't have any money to use and I didn't know where to get the money, so I had to figure out a way to buy real estate WITHOUT money! The system in which I was following showed me how I could buy a property without money, so instead of just doing it one time, I repeated the cycle over and over again! ☺ Owner financing became a specialty of mine. This is where the owners will carry the financing of the home (no bank qualifying) and sell to me on terms (agreement for deed or with a note/mortgage). I would market to people that had real estate to sell but wasn't selling as fast as they needed it to sell. In other words, the property could be costing them money per month, need repairs, be sitting vacant, or maybe even have no equity, all in which was very inconvenient for them! My solution would ease their 'pain' and create a win/win/win for all parties. What I mean by this is that I would buy the home, taking the burden off their hands. I would have a property which didn't cost me any money, and I could market this home to someone as a rental, rent to own, or land contract. They would put money down or have a fee to move in with which would = profit for me! So – the seller won, the buyer (me) won, and the person moving in won! When you look out for everyone else in the transaction and not just yourself, it is amazing how the 'warm & fuzzies' will not only increase your referral business, BUT you feel amazing about helping others! Focus on others' success, and you will be amazed as to how quickly it comes back to you! ☺

Since you will be learning so much in your new venture, your business will begin to take on different looks. There will be new vocabulary and brand-new ways to increase your business right before your eyes. You get to choose - Yet another neat thing about real estate investing. If you love people, you can deal directly with them. If you decide to deal more with numbers and banks, you can do that, too. This will allow you to live a life by design rather than by default. I also know people that start with real estate because everywhere you look, there is opportunity. But they use this as a vehicle to get the cash they need to do something else that makes them happy! The possibilities are really endless; the people you meet along your journey will empower you to move beyond your wildest expectations!

During my discovery and growth process, as I call it, I realized that the system I had always used wasn't really geared toward what my business looked like today. It had been four years and 120 + houses with 300 transactions, and I nor my business were the same as when I started. You will have these moments yourself when you begin to grow and change, and then it will be time to adapt to a new system that better fits how things are today, as well as your new knowledge!

This is where finding Lou Brown – King of Cash Flow - supercharged my business from where I was to where I am now headed! Not only does Lou have a great system to follow, but he is also a pure genius at deal structuring and expanding your business to the next level! Becoming a Certified Affordable Housing Provider provided the system and credibility to expand the property management side of the business. Having a stair-step plan approach to potential clients, marketing to their ability to start at one level and move up to the next, empowering clients to have a chance at homeownership that they didn't realize they had, was a perfect partner in what we were currently doing. The credibility of the system and fellow CAHP's located around the world provided such a new angle for our business that we had not perfected on our own. There is power in a system – in numbers – and in associations that you aren't able to accomplish without others. Clients that are new to your business that you haven't already built a reputation with are drawn to the system and association that there are more than one of you. This helps them feel comfortable with you.

Success Stories

Offering our homes to clients that will empower them to become homeowners when they least expected they would qualify is what makes you feel good about what you do. Not only did I have a desire to change my financial situation, find a schedule of my own where I could be a Mom, and being a blessing to others really sealed the deal for me. Our clients have allowed us to not only be blessed but be a blessing to them (that is a big deal for me – I'm not in this to be all about me!). These people and stories keep me going when I get down, have a bad week or month, become overwhelmed, and feel like giving up. I remind myself of just how important this is to them and their families as well ☺

Such as the Camp family – He is in his 40's, and he and his wife had never had an opportunity to move into a home of their own with the possibility of owning it one day. He was so proud, he took the sign out of the ground and held it high and took a picture with it so he could show his Mom he 'finally' did it! Or the story of Dawn and her husband, she being on disability and he from Canada with no social security number – no one would give them a chance to move into their home much less an opportunity to own it one day – they tell us every month how they love their home! Or Betty, who had lost her husband and was living in the home all by herself for two years while it was listed and didn't sell. She called in a panic that she couldn't afford any repairs if something went wrong and she was literally making herself sick worrying about it. She wanted so badly to go to an apartment and rest easy at night and not worry about repairs and upkeep. We bought her property on terms (as I mentioned earlier) and she was able to use these monthly payments to pay her apartment. She was so pleased – we even helped her move! Oh yes, then there is Alvin. We had a home that needed repairs (it was actually condemned the day we bought it) and we weren't in a position to put in all of those repairs. We offered the home to him on Agreement for Deed, where he could make payments to us until paid in full. He would fix it with his own money, the way he wanted to. He was so happy; no one had ever given him that opportunity before. The home is now livable, off the condemned list, and he's made a great home for him and friends! Then there is Mikki – she needed at least 18 months before she would qualify for a traditional bank mortgage. She fell in love with one of our homes and we offered her Rent to Own (lease option) until she could qualify for the mortgage.

These are just a few of our stories that help us to feel good about what we do – about what we offer to others. We strongly feel that everyone deserves a home of their own, regardless of their past credit issues. We feel just as strongly about sellers as we do buyers. We really are here to help those that have real estate issues. As you learn and grow yourself, your toolbox begins to grow as well – allowing you the different tools to use to solve their real estate issues. What you know today will most definitely not be the same tomorrow!

Increasing your dollars and helping others

The last thing I want to share with you before closing has been so exciting to us! We have been able to help many people earn more money on their investment dollars than what they were earning before! For example: Many people have IRA's, 401k's, or savings in the bank where they are earning a low 3% (or even less) on their investment dollars!

Doing Good While Doing Well

Literally you earn a higher rate of return while your dollars are used to help buy foreclosed and abandoned properties, get them repaired, and place deserving families on the Path To Home Ownership! This is truly what it's all about ... helping your own family by having your money work harder – and helping other families in the meantime. This has been a very rewarding process on many levels!

What a few families had to say about our program:

> *"Shelly, I am so glad I invested my money with you. The returns are so much better than what I was getting in the bank! Thank you!"* (Tom, Los Angeles)

> *"Shelly Buys Houses! gave me the opportunity to make a lot more money on my savings without worrying it would disappear because of a bad economy. The loan was secured by real estate, so I knew I would get my money back, plus interest. What more could you ask for..... low risk, high returns, and no work on my part!"* (Carolyn, North Carolina)

In ending this chapter, I want to encourage you to follow your dreams! Set goals for yourself, read what others are doing, find a mentor, and most importantly... never give up! I have learned so much from Lou Brown and his Mastermind coaching – it has caused me to think bigger than I was (yes, that is possible LOL) and has pushed me beyond my comfort zone (which is where we grow the most!) I am truly grateful!

In whatever you decide to do – do it with all you've got and be blessed on your journey! ☺

About Shelly Fonner

Shelly Fonner is now married with five children and currently resides in Indiana, where she started in 2008 and continues to build her business of real estate! Frank, her husband, joined her in the business, and the 'kids' can't wait to get a piece of the action when they get older!

When recently interviewed, Shelly shared 5 important ingredients for changing your life. Having met every challenge and obstacle along her journey, she states that you have not failed unless you refuse to get back up! "Many people that have fulfilled their purpose in life have fallen down numerous times... the moral of the story is to be sure you get up one more time than you fall down!"

1) Positive Thoughts = Positive Actions = Positive Results! You cannot put negative in and expect positive out... What you think about and talk about- You bring about... choose your thoughts carefully!!

2) Find a successful system and follow it! You do not know what you do not know... find a system that teaches what you want to do and follow it!

3) Network group – Find like-minded people and hang out with them! Share ideas, concepts, talk about your business! Many times you will hear "If you want to see what your future will look like – look around at the company you keep!"

4) Study the habits of the Rich as compared to the Poor! Successful people do common things differently... Copy what successful people do and implement it as your own!

5) Take action! You can learn all you want to learn but if you never do anything with your knowledge, it will be wasted!

Create your life by design, and go for it! You deserve to live your life on purpose and impact others on your way! You and I were never meant to be mediocre! Doubt kills more dreams than failure ever will.... (Stop being doubtful and start believing in yourself!)

Shoot for the moon and if you fall short, you will still land among the stars!

Follow Shelly on Facebook & Twitter and visit **www.ShellyBuysHouses.com** for direct links to social media and other sites! ☺

Shelly has proudly received the following certifications and awards:

- Community Affordable Housing Provider PLATINUM award from the GD Sanford Foundation
- Certified Affordable Housing Provider (CAHP)
- Certified Deal Specialist
- Certified Trust Specialist
- Building Wealth Hall of Fame

Chapter 10

The Win-Win Solution

By Kevin and Cynthia Shriver

*"A win-win attitude plus a win-win situation equals
a Win-Win Solution!"*

Win-Win Solutions Trust is a private Real Estate Investing Company formed in May 2007 to acquire, rehabilitate, lease or resell residential real estate. The co-managers of the company are Cynthia Shriver and Kevin Shriver, who have experience in real estate investing since 1989. The goal of the company is to provide affordable housing in Madison County, Illinois and the surrounding areas.

The mission statement of our company is *"We Transform Lives Through Affordable Housing to Empower Families and Individuals to Enjoy the American Dream of Home Ownership!"* The initial focus of the company was to acquire homes in which the homeowner was on the brink of foreclosure and offer them some credit bruising relief by negotiating a short sale with their Lender. This offered a winning scenario for the homeowner and provided inventory for the company in which the company could offer affordable housing to new or existing homeowners. As the years passed, we understood that many of our buying customers, while wanting to own their own home, had economic, employment or credit problems which kept them from qualifying for a traditional mortgage loan. Because we quickly recognized that demand, the business was expanded to include offering affordable, single-family housing to folks that might not initially qualify for traditional bank loans.

Through the Certified Affordable Housing Provider (CAHP) licensing and extensive training program, Win-Win Solutions Trust has implemented creative home purchase financing techniques such as Agreement For Deed, or Lease Purchase Agreement, which allows Customers/Buyers to make an initial down payment or option deposit while occupying the home. This allows our Customers/Buyers to make progress toward homeownership. They may even begin the homeownership process by renting the home. While living in what will eventually be their own home, our Customers/Buyers can build equity, repair their credit, establish a reputable financial management history and ultimately become qualified for a standard home mortgage. This model also gives our customers a financial incentive to maintain their properties. We even offer a work-for-equity credit, which can be used as a portion of the down payment toward the home purchase.

Through these programs, Customers/Buyers will pay a down payment or option fee along with monthly payments, giving these Customers/Buyers the time and opportunity to increase their ability to secure a traditional home mortgage from a bank or other financial institution. We have also helped customers to take advantage of the down payment assistance (10% of the purchase price or $8,000 maximum) offered by the Obama administration in 2009/10. This truly helped the homeowner jump-start the down payment amount to lower their monthly payments.

Additionally, we offer to our Customer/Buyers that are in the *"Path To Home Ownership (PTHO)"* program assistance repairing their bruised credit, enabling them to be better positioned to obtain their own traditional mortgage. Having these customers fulfill the dream of homeownership, along with their improved credit, allows the local economy to flourish with their improved spending power. For these customers, the pride of homeownership enhances the stability of neighborhoods and the family unit. The PTHO program is typically a 1-3 year program with progressive incentives toward eventual homeownership via traditional lending mechanisms. While most of our customers complete the program within this time frame, we have instances of families that complete the process in as little as 6 months.

Doing Good While Doing Well

Our Customers/Buyers understand and appreciate that Win-Win Solutions Trust has demonstrated a strong commitment to parts of the community whose housing needs have been badly underserved, and where few realistic options have been available to those seeking and capable of homeownership. Win-Win Solutions Trust not only provides affordable housing, but also by the very nature of the business helps the local economy by providing work for local contractors, realtors, mortgage companies, building suppliers, and other related businesses.

We are a customer service driven business. We will go the extra mile to help homeowners to improve their credit not only by providing a credit repair service that also provides bank financing when the time is right, but additionally, we dedicate extra effort to remind customers of on-time bill payments and develop strategies with the customer to ensure it.

Being customer-driven has provided *Win-Win Solutions Trust* opportunities to help individuals in unique circumstances. One such instance involved a handicapped couple who were struggling with a home payment they could no longer afford, which led them to become behind in their payments. Through our program we were able to purchase their home, freeing them of this debt, and then were able to re-sell the home to an individual that needed housing upon being released from prison. This individual wanted a fresh start in society and was not offered such an opportunity via a traditional lending path. We were able to help him own a home once again.

Win-Win Solutions Trust is able to find homes which are made available to our PTHO customers in a variety of ways. One method we employ to find homes is to help sellers that need to sell their home and have been unsuccessful via traditional marketing methods. The company also purchases homes via Estate sales or auctions where families find themselves burdened with an unwanted home from a family member. And finally, we purchase homes for the PTHO buyers as foreclosed properties being sold by HUD or a banking institution. The homes are selected for purchase based on our database of PTHO buyers and match a home based on their identified financial and physical needs for a home.

Our company uses different techniques to make affordable housing available in the marketplace. An Agreement for Deed contract is established by setting up installment payments. In the case of such a contract between a purchaser and a seller, the seller holds legal title of a property, while at the same time financing the sale price of the property to a purchaser. Up until the debt is paid in full, the Seller will hold the legal title to the property.

The fact that no deed passes hands is the primary difference between a standard deed of trust and an Agreement for Deed. A buyer can continue making payments after taking possession of the property. Remember, possession is not the same thing as ownership. Once the balance is paid in full, or earlier if the Company decides to, we will then record the deed, thereby passing title to the buyer.

This is an alternate method of financing in a time when money is tight and qualifying for credit can be difficult, or even impossible, for many potential home-buyers. Conventional loan processing situations usually call for more processing hindrances and higher closing costs. If the buyer defaults on payments, the seller still retains all payments and clear title because he or she still retains legal title and the deed to the property.

Another Win-Win situation for both the Seller and the Buyer is that the Agreement for Deed contract benefits both the Seller and home buyer because the buyer can buy the property without having to qualify for a loan, and the Seller can hold on to the title to the property. The Buyer has all the benefits of any other homeowner, including tax deductions.

The Company uses funds borrowed from private lenders to invest in real estate primarily, but not necessarily exclusively, in and around Madison County, Illinois. *Win-Win Solutions Trust* focuses on residential properties. The team makes it our business to keep an eye on business developments in the real estate markets. We believe it benefits us and our private lenders to do so, and it also helps us manage the risks of, and increases the odds of, succeeding in our investment strategy. This allows for a winning strategy for our private lenders that are afforded an opportunity to earn much higher rates of return on their money without higher risk.

Currently one of our Private Lenders has 7 different loans with us and has a goal to have at least 12 in order to receive an interest payment monthly; an interest payment for each month of the year. This lender is so confident in our CAHP / PTHO program that this has become a big part of their monthly and retirement income stream. The company also has Private Lenders that are using their IRAs and ROTH IRAs to build their retirement accounts faster with safe, higher rates of return on their money. They were looking for diversification in their investing without exposing themselves to the ups/downs of the stock market or the ridiculously low CD rates and money market funds that do not keep up with inflation. This form of investment is also appealing to elderly, retirement age individuals in that we currently have several lenders that are looking for stable, steady, fixed interest payments on their investment dollars at multiple times the interest rate currently paid by CDs and money market funds without the risk of the stock market. We feel so strongly about protecting our Private Lenders' investments that we created a Private Placement Memorandum (PPM) in 2011 that was submitted to the United States Securities and Exchange Commission (SEC) per Regulation D, Rule 506 of the Securities Act of 1933, as amended. Our Private Lenders find themselves in a winning investment strategy with our program.

Win-Win Solutions Trust currently manages double-digit numbers of properties that have numerous customers on the Path to Home Ownership at a variety of levels … some have started at renting, some are Lease-Option, and others are Agreement for Deed. Members on this "Path" can begin at any level and skip levels while working toward homeownership. Moving to the next level involves increased down payment amounts, while improving their credit. These members are usually in the program from 1 to 3 years, with the ultimate goal of traditional bank financing and lowered monthly payments within that time frame.

Not only is *Win-Win Solutions Trust* in the business of helping more people become homeowners, the company also helps private lenders (individuals) earn more money on their un-invested funds and/or improve the growth of their self-directed IRAs, as well as assisting home Sellers that may need a non-traditional way in which to sell their home. As an example, we were able to help a family that wanted to sell their home. They had it for sale in the local MLS but were unable to sell it. They needed to be closer to family members that were out of the area to help with their small children. We were able to buy their home, freeing them to move closer to their family, on a time table that met with their needs. At nearly the same time the family moved from this home, a new family, which is a member of the *Path To Home Ownership* program, moved in and is on their journey to homeownership.

In another instance, we were able to help a seller that had moved out of the home and had moved their son into the property until the son had a job transfer to Texas. The seller attempted to market the property for sale via traditional means for 8 months. The seller was fearful of damage from renting the property, so the property was vacant during this time. We were able to offer the seller an agreed-upon price which allowed him to stop the monthly costs of a home that provided no source of income and that he no longer wanted. Another Win-Win solution!

There are numerous other families that we have helped avoid foreclosure by structuring short-sales with their lenders, thereby avoiding a foreclosure on their credit report. We have also been able to help some of these same people that have lost their home to a short-sale or foreclosure through our PTHO program.

The company also looks for ways in which to give back to the community with its knowledge of Real Estate transactions, mortgage lending, and insurance companies …. One such instance was involving an elderly gentleman that approached our company to purchase his home. Upon further investigation, it was found that this man owed a minimal remaining amount on his mortgage. However, he felt trapped with having to sell his home due to a leaking roof, damage from a fire, and other needed repairs, yet without the financial means to have the repairs done. In the midst of this dilemma, he was a bit behind on the small amount remaining on his mortgage. Due to this arrearage of his payments, the lender would not release the funds provided by the insurance carrier for the covered fire damage. *Win-Win Solutions Trust* coordinated with the lender to use the insurance proceeds to pay off the remaining mortgage balance and return the overage to the homeowner. We then made arrangements with a local not-for-profit organization to have the roof and fire damage repaired, and the whole interior of the home cleaned. Through these efforts, this elderly gentleman was able to stay in his now completely paid off and repaired home without any cost to him. A tremendous Win-Win solution for everyone involved.

Primary operations of our company are managed by 2 co-managers and a number of contracted businesses for specific services. Day-to-day operations include the following:

- Working with PTHO customers to match their financial and physical needs of a home
- Working with Sellers that need to sell their home
- All services associated with property management of PTHO program homes

- General contracting services for individual contractors of the following disciplines:
  - HVAC installation and servicing
  - Plumbing installation and repair
  - Electrical installation and repair
  - Flooring and ceramic tile installation
  - General carpentry
  - Painter
  - Roofing installation / repair
  - Specialists for hardwood floor restoration, plastering repair, sewer clean-out
  - Coordinated services with Credit Repair company and associated Lender for PTHO customers
- Working with new Private Lenders in order to expand the number of homes and number of families we can help
- Title company coordination
- Real Estate Agent services
- Contracting services with Certified Public Accountants
- Contracting services with Legal Counsel
- Continuing education training to offer the best of services to our customers (Sellers and Buyers), suppliers, private lenders, contractors, and the local community

In these operations, the company **Win-Win Solutions Trust** was founded and embodies on a daily basis the philosophy of always doing business with customers, suppliers, private lenders, contractors, and the community with a "Win-Win" objective.

About Kevin and Cynthia Shriver

Kevin & Cynthia were high school sweethearts growing up about 5 miles apart in rural Illinois. After graduating from separate colleges, Cynthia from University of Illinois and Kevin from Illinois State University, they married in 1982. They have been involved in real estate investing since 1989.

Both Kevin & Cynthia have had extensive training in the *Street Smart System* and have completed the requirements for Certified Trust Specialist, Certified Income Specialist, and Certified Deal Specialist. They are members of the Certified Affordable Housing Program (CAHP), as well as the Platinum coaching program for three years. In Jan 2012, they received the Community Affordable Housing Provider Silver Award from the GD Sanford Foundation.

To learn more about how **Win-Win Solutions Trust** can help you, visit their websites at:

www.PrettyHomeForYou.com

www.WinWinHomeSale.com

www.WinningInvestmentForYou.com

"*For evil to flourish, all that is needed is for good people to do nothing.*"

~Edmund Burke~

Chapter 11

Helping Deserving Families

Darren Fettik

"The purpose of life is not to be happy. It is to be useful, to be honorable, to be compassionate, to have it make some difference that you have lived and lived well." ~Ralph Waldo Emerson~

Since 1998 I have owned a car customization business. Back then I had a partner who had a ton of Carlton Sheets cd's. When I asked him what they were, he explained that they were real estate books. Being the over-achiever that I am, I started listening to them. They were cd's on how to buy properties. Within two years I bought eight properties. Good job, right?

Not really.

You see, even though I learned how to buy properties, I didn't learn how to *manage* properties. The tenants were running all over me. They would vandalize the houses, steal whatever wasn't bolted down, (and a few things that were) refuse to pay rent and then squat. I eventually learned how to evict them but at some point I became disenchanted and eventually, I let the properties go.

Doing Good While Doing Well

I still knew that real estate was the right thing for me, but I had to find the right niche. So for about a year and a half I started taking classes, aggressive marketing techniques. I spent over $100,000 on these classes, but they just didn't seem right after a time. Then I joined the Certified Affordable Housing Provider® network. I realized that there was a lot better approach to finding properties. I have been consistently taking continuing educational classes, and what a difference! It all makes sense to me now.

What I really enjoy is helping deserving families become buyers and the Path to Home Ownership® program. I think it's an AMAZING program! It helps everybody get on the right track. We help them finance the property. We help them repair their credit or fix their debt to income ratio, whatever their qualifying issue may be that they need to overcome. It's very satisfying helping people that normally wouldn't qualify for traditional loans have the opportunity to actually qualify for a loan. One of the first tenants that I worked with is just so excited to not only be in a house they love but know that they can actually own it. So right now they are on the Path to Home Ownership® program and going through the steps of getting their credit repaired and working towards the bank financing. It's a great opportunity for them.

It's really satisfying for me when I see a tenant willing to work and do some rehab on a house, knowing that if they work really hard, the house will become theirs.

I recently had a family come to me and say that they had somebody that was supposed to do a rent-to-own on their house, and then out of the blue, the landlord decided to sell the house outright and gave them a few months to get out of the house. They were pretty upset about it. I took them to see a house and as they were walking the property, the whole family was really getting excited. They said they could do all the work that was needed. As I write this, they are actually doing the work on the property. They haven't moved into it yet because as per our contract, they can't move in until they get the work done. But they are working on it as quickly as they can. It's very gratifying to see the whole family pull together and work towards this new chapter in their lives.

A lot of the process is about the pride of ownership. It's not only good for my clients, but also for the entire neighborhood. I know that once they get the house finished that they will upkeep it. It gives them a totally different mindset when they have to work hard to achieve something that valuable.

I get the enjoyment of making them homeowners. I also get to improve the neighborhood and, of course, make a profit. At this point my goal is to manage 100 occupied properties in the next couple of years. From the beginning I self-funded, but now I am looking to investors to help defray the cost. The lenders, during that process, get a very secure investment and an above-average return to what they could get elsewhere, so it's a no-brainer to many.

I've also talked to people about using their IRA's or other retirement funds for financing. They are finding that the interest isn't all that good, and we can sometimes triple the return. We can offer them diversification, which a lot of the brokerage houses cannot. The risk is minimal because they're on a first lien position and the property is controlled by an educated, experienced investor, so it makes it a pretty safe investment for them. They can even transfer their current IRA to a self-directed IRA to achieve a higher interest rate.

An Early Entrepreneur

When I was 11 years old and growing up in Buffalo, NY, one of my friends had a paper route that he wanted to give up. So I said I wanted it. One of the managers came over to my house to sign me up but when he found out I was only 11 years old, he was ready to walk away. I begged him and said I really wanted this paper route. Finally he said, "Well, I'm just going to go ahead and put down that you're 12 and then that way you get the paper route." So since the age of 11 I've been an entrepreneur. I was selling gum, candy and blow pops in school and I was babysitting at nighttime after classes in addition to my paper route and a couple of other jobs.

Many people don't know the extent of my business expertise over and above my real estate expertise. My background helps me run my company efficiently and allows it to grow fast.

Like I stated earlier, in 1998 I started a car audio business. Throughout the years it has grown to more of a car customization business. We do vehicle wraps, window tint, vehicle security systems, TVs, navigation systems, advertising print wraps, signs, banners, etc. Since I first opened the doors I have grown the business to 11 employees. Audio Designs & Custom Graphics is a nationally recognized facility. We have been voted one of the Top 12 facilities in all of North America by Mobile Electronics Retailer magazine and voted the #1 shop in Jacksonville, FL, 3 years, by News4Jax.

Then in 2015 I separately partnered and co-founded a business named the Window Tint School. We have five different classrooms, and we're the only dedicated window tint school in the entire country. Now there are other schools that teach, but they're more like a retail facility. The students come in, and they work on whatever cars are there. Believe it or not, each car in different. Our school is really structured. We went to the junkyard and bought a bunch of different car doors. We have one room with just doors in it. It kind of gets aggressively harder. We teach them how to tint front windows, side windows and the back windows. Each window, depending on the make and model, can be tinted differently. We've had people from all over the world come to our classes to learn. We've had people from Haiti, Honduras, Canada, all over the U.S. It's a pretty cool experience.

So not only am I creating homeowners, I'm also creating a worldwide network of entrepreneurs.

I am very lucky in the fact that I have alternate cash flow coming in that I can use for investments and run my real estate business, but I also come with a lot of business background. I think that's important to investors. Even though they have the security of the property, the best security is knowing that they're working with a real professional.

About Darren Fettik

Darren Fettik received the mathematics award in high school for the highest math average of 4 years in a class of 425 students. He went on to be recognized as one of the smartest mathematics students by the head of the math department of the State University of New York at Potsdam. He was on the path to major in Actuarial Science when his entrepreneurial instincts kicked in and he started his car customization business. He loved working on cars and decided an office job just wasn't for him.

Darren has been involved with real estate since 1998. He has experience in wholesaling, rehabbing, flipping, short term (AirBNB) and long term rentals.

Darren has completed the requirements for Certified Trust Specialist, Certified Income Specialist, and Certified Deal Specialist. He is also a member of the Certified Affordable Housing Program® as well as a member of the Platinum Program.

In 2019, his company, Coast To Coast Properties, received the Community Affordable Housing Provider Bronze award from the G.D. Sanford Foundation, an award that honors those companies who have adopted the philosophy and programs to deliver safe, affordable housing in their local communities by placing deserving families into the Path To Home Ownership Program®.

If you are looking to purchase a home through our Path to Home Ownership Program®, sell a home, or are looking to invest to receive a good secure return, Darren can be reached by phone, **904-417-7699**, email, **Darren@CtoCproperties.com** or visit **www.904HomeSellers.com** or **www.904HomeBuyers.com**.

Our Mission Is To Transform Lives Through Affordable Housing To Empower Families And Individuals To Enjoy The American Dream Of Home Ownership

Chapter 12

One At A Time

By Todd Haring

"When everything seems to be going against you, remember that the airplane takes off against the wind, not with it." – Henry Ford

Even as a young boy, I was passionate about real estate. I find homeownership instills a level of certainty and comfort in people's lives; mine included. Even the name implies that there is something special about it; after all, it has the word "real" built right into it. Something about the building of real property, the remodeling of real property, and the investing/managing of real property has always felt just right to me.

As a young man, I've always wanted to take houses that needed some TLC and breathe new life back into them. Back in 1986, when I was 23 years old, I bought my first multi-unit. It was a two-unit and I lived in one unit and rented out the other.

Over the years I have literally had my hands involved with real estate in one way or another. For example, I am also an electrician by trade. I have done electrical and handyman types of jobs on both residential and commercial construction, ranging from brand new to very old buildings. In addition, I ran my own successful electrical construction business for years.

Specialized Knowledge

I've always had a thirst for specialized knowledge. I believe that the more knowledge and experience I have, the more I can effectively help others achieve what they want. Today, one of my specialties is helping homeowners who are behind on their mortgage payments and/or property taxes. Even if a homeowner has no equity (or even negative equity) in their house, I can usually help them.

I enjoy not only helping people that have a house to sell, but I also enjoy helping deserving families and individuals achieve the American dream of homeownership. Pride of homeownership is a real thing. That's why Trust Valley Properties offers the Path to Home Ownership® (PTHO) program. Approximately 70% - 80% of people who want to own a home of their own do not qualify to purchase a house in the traditional manner (going to a bank to get a loan). The PTHO program is designed to help deserving families and individuals achieve the American Dream of homeownership, regardless of their credit or financial background.

"Comps"

Comps (Comparable houses that have sold) are a vital tool of the trade. Without comps, how can anybody accurately determine the value of a house? In the past, the only way to have access to reliable comps was through the Multiple Listing Service (MLS). And the only way to have access to the MLS was to be a Realtor. So, in 1992, I became a Realtor, with the sole intent of being a real estate investor (not a Realtor). Since then a lot has obviously changed with technology and the internet. Fortunately, today, there is no need for anybody to be a Realtor simply to have access to comps.

The Disillusionment

During the time I was a Realtor, I inadvertently discovered that the psychology of a Realtor and the psychology of a real estate investor are, in many respects, exact opposites of each other. I was shocked to hear many Realtors saying the last thing they would ever do is invest in real estate. How crazy is that?

Now, I want to make it perfectly clear that I do have respect for Realtors.

They provide a service for the "typical" house seller and house buyer. But what about the seller or buyer that is not "typical"? What if the...

- Seller does not have enough equity in the house to pay for the Realtor commissions and other closing costs?
- Seller's house needs repairs and the seller does not have the funds or time to do the required repairs?
- Seller needs to sell quickly?
- Seller needs immediate debt relief?
- Seller cannot afford to make the monthly mortgage payments on house until it sells?
- Buyer does not have good enough credit to get a mortgage from a bank?
- Buyer does not have enough cash for the down payment and closing costs?
- Buyer is self-employed and cannot qualify for a bank loan?
- Buyer's banker drags the loan commitment process out a very long time, through no fault of the buyer?
- Buyer can't get a bank mortgage because the banks are in financial trouble themselves?

Branding

I did, however, learn a valuable lesson through being both a Realtor and owning my own electrical construction business. Branding is critical in today's world of business! For better or for worse, the psychology of the consumer has changed. There was a time when a person could start their own "Ma & Pa" business, and the consumer would respect that. But in today's environment, that is not enough. Consumers today are much more inclined to do business with a company that is associated with a quality group of like-minded individuals (such as an "association"). This is where branding comes in.

Doing Good While Doing Well

When I first learned about the CAHP program, it made perfect sense to me, and it felt like I was home. I knew it was a great way to demonstrate that we are not your typical "We Buy Houses" company. To become a Certified Affordable Housing Provider® requires specialized training and testing. That's one of the many reasons why I was immediately sold on the CAHP brand and the PTHO program.

Today, it is simply not enough just to be competent. A service provider needs to demonstrate that they are competent. It's important to brand your business. My branding is the CAHP program and the PTHO program. I know how to help people with a house to sell. I also know how to match that house to the right deserving family or individual and structure it so the home buyer can afford the house. Many times, this means Trust Valley Properties will finance (act as the bank) the property to the happy homeowners. Deserving home buyers are deeply grateful for the opportunity to be on the Path to Home Ownership®.

Consumers today feel more comfortable doing business with people that are held to a higher standard. What the brand of "Realtor" is to a real estate agent, "Certified Affordable Housing Provider" (CAHP) is to me, a real estate investor/manager. With the CAHP program, we are in our own business, but we are not in business on our own. There is a quality support team behind us.

Our Mission Statement

"We transform lives through affordable housing to empower families and individuals to enjoy the American dream of homeownership."

Our Code of Ethics

Being a Certified Affordable Housing Provider® also means having higher standards, such as our code of ethics. As a CAHP, our intent is to:

- Help Sellers get a quick and efficient sale

- Help Buyers and Renters get affordable housing
- Help Private Lenders use their funds and get good returns while helping provide more affordable housing for others
- Help the community with affordable housing needs
- Be lawful
- Be courteous
- Act with integrity in all matters
- Be an excellent team player
- Do the right thing
- Protect our amazing win-win brand

The Home Buyer's Aspirations

Recent studies indicate the following regarding American homeownership...

- People still want to achieve the American Dream of homeownership, yet they struggle financially to attain it.
- Homeownership leads to an *increase* in graduation rates, children's good health and net family wealth.
- Homeownership leads to a *decrease* in children's behavioral problems and reliance on government assistance.

Can we, as a local community, make a positive difference in other people's lives through affordable housing? For generations to come?

As Certified Affordable Housing Providers®, we believe we can, one at a time.

About Todd Haring

Todd Haring was born and raised in the Lehigh Valley area of Pennsylvania. His entrepreneurial spirit started at an early age. While he was still in elementary school, he had ambition as he did minor jobs for his neighbors, such as mowing lawns, raking leaves, shoveling snow, and delivering the Evening Chronical (a second newspaper The Morning Call used to print back in the day). While attending High School, he attended a Vocational Technical School where he learned the construction trades and majored in the electrical construction trade. After graduating from High School, he continued his education on construction, real estate and mortgage notes by attending many various classes.

Over the past 40+ years, he has had vast experience in purchasing, remodeling, managing, and selling real estate. To this day, he continues his real estate education with subjects ranging from construction, property management, business management, finances and more.

Today, Todd has expanded to reach more of his "neighbors" as he manages a friendly community-based real estate investing business. He buys, sells, rents, and manages real property in the Lehigh Valley area of Pennsylvania.

For a free no-obligation consultation, please reach out to Todd and see how he and the Trust Valley Properties team can help you with your unique house selling and/or buying needs.

Doing Good While Doing Well

www.TrustValleyProperties.com

Manager@TrustValleyProperties.com

24 Hour Recorded Message: 610-456-2052

Mobile: 610-465-7355

"*What I hear, I forget.*

What I see, I remember.

What I do, I know."

~Chinese proverb~

Chapter 13

It's Never Too Late to Write
the Next Chapter of Your Life

Robert Slye

"Discipline is the bridge between goals and accomplishment."
~Jim Rohn~

My story started back around 1987. I bought my first rental property and I was in the middle of that rehab and thinking, "What did I get myself into?" I was a pipe fitter at a GM plant and I wanted to invest in properties on the side because I saw that there were lots of advantages to the real estate business as far as creating cash flow, capital gains, having deep appreciation and deductions to shelter income. Sounds viable, right?

Well, at that time I didn't have any systems in place. I was working a "real job" so it was a little messy at times because I'm more of a hands on person than an organizer. However, at one point I had five doubles and two singles that I managed. I also had a few others along the way. I sold everything in the early 2000s and I was debt free. I decided to invest my money into a nice house that I could enjoy. I figured that the appreciation on that big number would grow even faster and that I would start doing more flips with my equity line to pay that house off. When I retired I would sell that house and pay cash for a new downsized house and put the rest in the bank. But you know, life's plans go awry sometimes and they closed our plant in 2006.

My wife and I both worked at the plant so we both lost our jobs. The market crash came, we divorced, and I had to sell our house at a loss. The only good thing that came out of this triple whammy was that I got custody of my daughter, who was eight at the time. Raising her by myself, I knew I needed to put things in order and do something fast. I needed to support her. Luckily, I knew from my experience in real estate that it was a great way to help people in the community, as well as making a financial path for myself and my daughter. Since I didn't have any capital to work with, I started doing home repairs. I was a pipe fitter and had an HVAC design degree. So I printed up 25 flyers and my daughter and I went around the neighborhood and passed them out. I got three jobs immediately. Neighbors were referring me and I kept working. I then started a home inspection business and joined a local REIA group to network and hopefully get some home inspection jobs.

While at the REIA meetings I listened and learned quite a bit. Even though I wanted to get back into real estate investing, I didn't see it in happening in my foreseeable future. But I learned how my IRA could work for me. I was already familiar with self-directed IRAs and I did have money in an IRA. So I rolled it over and did my first deal with my IRA. I made good money, but it all went back into my IRA. None of it went into my pocket. I needed to find a way to do deals without my own money.

Along the way I took a lot of courses. I wanted the best business model I could find so that I could teach and employ my daughter, have her enjoy the benefits of a successful business, and leave her a legacy. While I was taking one of these courses, part of the deal was a free course with Lou Brown in his Trust System. I wish I had met him first. His Path To Home Ownership® and Certified Affordable Housing Program® was a perfect model for what I was looking for. It's a complete system. It's a way to help people make a good income. And more importantly, it's a brand we're building. It's nationwide, so it gives us a lot more credibility.

One of the things I like about Lou's programs is that he teaches us to find the buyer first. If you have your buyer, you know what to look for when you're buying homes. From your list of buyers' needs, you know that you will have a client that will match what you buy. Before when I would rehab a property I felt like I was in control all the way up to when it was time to put it on the market. Then I just had to sit there and wait for a buyer to come along. I don't have to wait anymore since I find the buyer first.

Another reason why I like his program is because I can help people who never thought they could buy a home actually buy one. I can talk to them about different ways to purchase their new home - from rent, rent to own, to seller financing. This allows us to find a home that meets their needs and is affordable.

Lou's system teaches us to buy off market. So we market to sellers who are either out of state owners or non-owner occupied homes; who are generally tired landlords. Many times they are inherited properties, usually need work, and they can't sell the traditional way. Many times they are willing to do owner financing, which actually allows us to pay them a little bit more. So it's satisfying to help them. They get rid of a property they don't want and one they don't want to put any money into fixing up. Also, they don't really know what to do with it. For example, I recently sold a property I bought from an out of state owner. He actually lived in the property before he moved out of state.

He had a local real estate company manage it for him and it just didn't turn out too well. It ended up sitting vacant for about a year and a half and needed a lot of work. I was able to buy it at a really good price and put about $25,000 in to it to fix it up. I had a total of about $100,000 in it and sold it for $149,900. That was a good deal. It helped him out because he was out of state and it was just a headache for him. He didn't have to worry about it anymore. I, as a buyer, made some money on it. Then, as a seller, I sold it to people who were able to buy a house that they otherwise couldn't have bought because they didn't have the funds or skills to fix it up.

Doing Good While Doing Well

Besides buyers, investors are another group of people we can help. We can usually help them get four to six times what they're earning currently. As I said earlier, as I rebuilt my life, I did my first deal out of my self-directed IRA. I didn't have the money to do deals and I knew other individuals that had money in the bank and it was earning less than 1%. So, I was able to help them take that money, they helped me fund my deals, and I helped them by paying them four to six times what they were earning. And it was secured by real estate. So I'm looking for more people to help who have uninvested funds or want a higher rate of return and want their investment secured by real estate. My investing website is **www.makemoneylikeabank.com.** I mean, how do you think banks make all that money?

They borrow at one rate and loan at a higher rate. So I'm able to pay these investors a higher rate than what they're getting elsewhere. And, it's secured by real estate. It's not risky, like the stock market where you have no real control. So we help the investors with a high rate of return. We help sellers get rid of unwanted properties and we help buyers by providing an affordable house that they can buy and maybe even do some of the work themselves to make it exactly what they want. That's why the name of the book is called Doing Good While Doing Well. We're helping all these people out, as well as their neighbors, by fixing up the property. In addition, property taxes are being paid again, and we're providing jobs for local stores and contractors.

While we create cash flows to fund our lifestyles, we can help others and build a business for our kids. I've always heard if you help enough other people get what they want, you'll get what you want. And here in Columbus, Ohio, right now there's like 400 people a week moving in. We're the 14th largest city in the country and occupancy rates are 98%. Rents are up, prices are up and all the new homes are starting at $300,000. There's nothing for the first-time home buyer or someone that needs something a little more affordable. And from the stats I've seen, we have about a 20,000 housing shortage for all the new people coming in over the next few years. So by me using the system that Lou created, I'm able to find these deals and work with buyers to buy their first home.

I'm looking forward to continually helping deserving families buy their first home in the next few years.

About Robert Slye

Robert Slye worked at GM as a pipe fitter for 28 years until they closed in 2006. He graduated with an Associates engineering degree in HVAC design and later on earned his bachelors of business degree. Currently a Certified Affordable Housing Provider®, Robert's passion is helping the people in his community attain their dream of homeownership.

As a member of his church, he has participated in 17 mission trips to Mexico, Venezuela, and Botswana.

Robert is a lifelong Buckeye, involved in sports all his life and currently does Ironman triathlons. He is the proud father of his artistic 19 year old daughter who's working with him in the business. He also is a member of his local REIA, COREE, which stands for Central Ohio Real Estate Entrepreneurs.

To learn more about how Robert can help you attain your dreams, visit:

Buyers website - **www.youdeserveahome.com**

Seller's website - **www.sellyourhomewithspeed.com**

Investing website - **www.makemoneylikeabank.com.**

Chapter 14

The Difference We Make

Victoria Washington and Tangela Slaton

We say "Yes" when most say "No."

My name is Victoria Washington. I currently operate my real estate company out of New York, NY, and Atlanta, GA.

I became intrigued with real estate when I was in high school. My mom was a realtor, and I loved going to see all the big houses. I was also very impressed by the large checks that she received when she sold a house. But more importantly, I loved how she helped others achieve the American dream of homeownership by being a liaison for the buyers.

Before I decided to follow in her footsteps and enter into the real estate world, I was wrapped up in the broadcasting world. I knew for sure that I wanted to be a broadcaster. At 21, I moved to NYC and worked at some of the top media companies, such as Sirius XM, Fox News, NBC, ABC, and local radio stations.

However, real estate was in my blood, and I just knew that the media field couldn't compete on many levels.

Real Estate eventually did become my life. When Introduced to the Affordable Housing Program through Lou Brown, I knew that it was in line with my beliefs on how people should be treated, how to help people become homeowners, and how to educate people about home ownership.

The Affordable Housing Program has opened up many doors for our clients by letting them know, as well as showing them that it is a better way to live and achieve the American dream. Wholesaling homes was a pretty decent living but working with clients who wanted and needed guidance through the Affordable Housing Program was way more satisfying.

Our clients come to us with a variety of situations, such as evictions, bad credit, foreclosures, previous homes burning down, the loss of jobs, minimal cash-flow, etc., etc. However, we work with everyone because our goal is to help each person who is an action-taker become a homeowner.

For example, we recently had a 45-year-old client who, due to unforeseen circumstances, was forced to move back in with her mother. Once she found our Affordable Housing Program, she was able to move into a starter home. Finding and using our program gave her peace of mind knowing she had her own place to call home.

Not only has the Affordable Housing Program improved other's lives, it also improved my life. I am able to get a different perspective on life and am able to create more ways to help others through employment, housing and community service.

I am not only providing affordable housing to families, but I am also showing others how to improve their lives with the methods I use to acquire homes to help our communities with housing.

Doing Good While Doing Well

My Name is Tangela Slaton. My journey into real estate began 20+ years ago. I was lucky to find a career that afforded me the opportunity to not only enjoy more family time together but to improve the quality of our lives.

I got started with the Path To Home Ownership™ Program (PTHO) because of my own life hurdles. Being a single mom of three was not easy. Most times it was a struggle. I knew that I wanted more for my babies. I remember going through the process of buying a home and then a short time later losing it. I was devasted. I did not have a plan. This program gives you a plan to succeed. After losing my home, no one would give me a fighting chance to start over. No one would meet me where I was in my life. I wanted to create better homeownership for myself and my children so that we could start building again. This program does that.

I love this program because it gives people like me, families and individuals a chance at homeownership now. A chance to live and be a part of the American Dream! It pushes people to not just want more but to act on it, to experience it, to live it.

This program creates homeowners. Once you've had that experience, it's hard to go back to the way things were. This program improves people's lives. This program makes our society better for everyone. This program gives other choices that they may not have had before. We are the community. We help build communities.

Let me tell you about a few of the clients that I have helped:

Doing Good While Doing Well

Seller 1: "Mary" and her husband were going through a divorce and she was starting her life over. Unfortunately, her husband was the sole provider as she had never held a job. After he left, she was on the verge of losing her home. Bankruptcy had failed her. Having a foreclosure would have made her new start very difficult. We were able to put her on the PTHO program, save her home and give her a fighting chance. She is now working and finding her independence with a new start in life.

Seller 2: "Sally's" husband of 10+ years had become both physically and verbally abusive. She was ready to leave and create a better life/future for her and the children. She needed to do this without alarming her husband. As she owned the home, we were able to help her transition safely to another residence without any incidents. In return, the seller wanted to pass it forward by giving another family a chance at homeownership with where they were in their life. The seller has since purchased a new home for herself and her children.

Buyer: This buyer touched my heart. She was a single mom and a dancer at a night club. Her current residence was being sold at auction in foreclosure. She had very little time to move her and her family. She was tired of being a renter and wanted to become a homeowner. She was very serious about securing her family with a home of their own. Within seven days of contacting us, she was able to move into her new home. Congratulations to her and her family!

I have met people that thought they would never become homeowners. They have lived in apartments all their lives. And in their minds, this was a way of life. It was all they knew. I have cried with people who just wanted to be a homeowner and just needed a chance.

This program allows all of this to be possible, and it's not only for 1st timers. It's for 2nd and 3rd timers, too. There will be instances when someone will need us more than once, and we will be there for them.

Doing Good While Doing Well

I love the Path To Home Ownership™ Program as it allows me to give others the chance that I was looking for. I just needed a helping hand, just like my clients.

My goal is to be of service to others so that I can make that difference in their lives.

Doing Good While Doing Well

About Victoria Washington

Victoria Washington has over ten years of real estate experience. She has a background in radio and TV, working in the number one market, New York City. Sirius XM Satellite Radio, Fox News Network, NBC Network, and ABC Network have taught her many things in the media world and how to leverage opportunities and help others along the way. Victoria enjoyed touching lives through the airwaves until she realized that she could do that same thing by providing affordable housing to the masses. Now, she is providing houses and helping others do the same in their own communities.

Find out more about what Victoria does at:

Info@NewOwnerNewStart.com

About Tangela Slaton

As a young mother of three, when **Tangela Slaton** worked in corporate America, it did not meet her measure of what success looked like. Working in a call center made it difficult to be available for her family. As her biological children were all transitioning into college, she decided to follow one of her childhood passions, which was to become a foster parent. She wanted to make a difference for our children in foster care. After serving many children, which she considers an honor, Tangela fostered four siblings who needed much of her attention.

Having a desire and an interest in Real Estate, she began her career as a Realtor. She knew then that helping others was very rewarding to her while providing for her family. There, her interest furthered into investing.

Tangela found interest in the Path To Home Ownership® Program. This program was everything she was looking for in real Estate. This program allows her to not only help buyers but to spend valuable time with her family.

For your house buying needs, contact Tangela at **678-280-2578, Ext 112** or **Tangela@NewOwnerNewStart.com.**

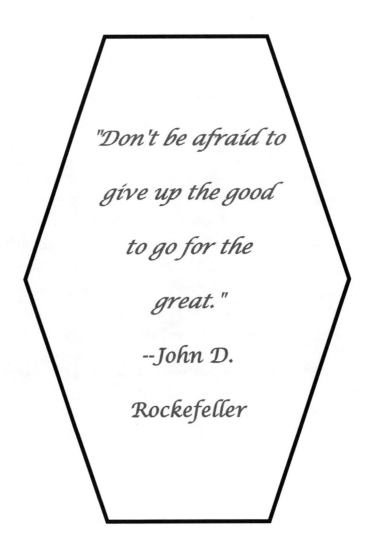

"Don't be afraid to give up the good to go for the great."
--John D. Rockefeller

Chapter 15

An Eye on Real Estate

Eddie and Valerie Coverson

"Not everything that is faced can be changed,

but nothing can be changed until it is faced." James Baldwin

Eagle Eye Home Solutions, LLC was founded in 2016. The premise of the business was built upon having an eagle-like vision about increasing home ownership. Eagles have very sharp vision. Compared to human sight, 20/20, an eagle's vision is 20/4. This means that they can see a lot clearer and sharper from 5 times as far as a human. We pride our business on being able to see clearly and offer clear solutions for homeowners. Eagles have two centers of vision which allow them to see two different directions. Eagle Eye Home Solutions, LLC similarly is able to see clearly to assist our sellers with the solutions they want and need in order to sell their house. We also have a clear vision to assist home buyers along their path towards home ownership. Here is our story.

Our foray into the real estate business happened by chance in 2010. We decided to purchase a new home to better accommodate our expanding family. It was a great time to buy, after the real estate market meltdown of 2008. However, due to those same conditions, it was a terrible time to sell a home! There was a drastic drop in home values and in spite of being fairly aggressive in paying our mortgage down for years, we soon learned that virtually all the equity we had worked so hard to gain had vanished. It was a great, well-kept house and we had lots of interest from people who wanted to make it theirs. Unfortunately, no one was willing to pay us what we wanted for the house and even if we found someone willing to pay our desired sale amount, surely no bank was going to approve a loan for what was now tens of thousands of dollars above the current home values for our neighborhood. Suddenly, we were stuck with a home that we could not afford to sell. Shortly after moving into our new home, around the same time as the novelty and excitement of our new place was beginning to wane, we unintendedly found ourselves trying to manage two mortgage payments and an empty house. While we were fortunate to be in a position to carry two mortgage payments for a period of time, we knew we could not maintain such an expense for the unforeseeable future. Thus, we had no other choice but to rent the house out and take a shot at landlording. It was through our first tenant that we learned of other families looking for stable homes in established neighborhoods. We also learned that plenty of those families are not able to go to a bank and qualify for a typical home loan for a myriad of reasons.

Becoming a first-time landlord was a learning curve. We learned through trial and error - some things we did right and other things we did wrong. Most importantly, we realized that we really did not know what we were doing. So that was one of the mechanisms that steered us into educating ourselves about real estate. We spent the next couple of years reading lots of real estate books, listening to webinars, attending seminars, and doing other forms of formal real estate training. Luckily, while on our journey to learning the real estate business, we eventually found Lou Brown and *Street Smart Systems*. With the right training and coaching, we were able to figure out the do's and don'ts of landlording and property management, but there were definitely some bumps and bruises along the way.

We did not let our rocky road into real estate investing deter us. Rather, we used it as a launching pad from which to grow. We saw the difference a stable home environment made to the families that we were assisting. We were also able to see gratitude from the families once they were able, with our guidance, to move on to purchase a home of their own. That is a rewarding experience! We consider all types of properties from move-in ready to fixer uppers as long as they meet the criteria that our clients need. You see, we meet with clients and look for homes based on their criteria. We concentrate on finding clients who want to become homeowners and treat them as such. We place them on *The Path to Home Ownership®*. We look for honest hard working people who want to become homeowners. We understand that there are good people who may not know where to start or who may have hit a few bumps on the road while on their journey to becoming a home owner. Our mission is to help bridge the gap, so our clients can achieve the American dream of home ownership. With our clients, we meet them wherever they are in their journey and we have options to work with everyone who desires home ownership, as long as they are coachable and willing to do what it takes to get there. We are able to work with clients on a rent level, rent-to-own level, and even provide in-house financing until they can qualify for a traditional bank loan. Along the way, we help them clean up their credit, learn to better manage their finances, build up their down-payment, etc. so they will have the best shot at becoming bank financeable.

We have learned that many people have no idea what it actually takes to own a home. We realize that people, especially first time home buyers in the communities in which we focus, often have never even lived in a single family home. In many cases, neither their parents, grandparents, nor anyone else in their immediate circle have ever owned a home. Realizing that if a lightbulb is out, or a water faucet has a slow drip, or the grass is too high, they can't just call the landlord, is a huge learning curve for them. They have to learn simple maintenance themselves. Our clients have to be willing to let go of the typical "renter" mentality and embrace a new way of thinking about where they live. We help our clients understand what it takes to qualify for a bank mortgage, including how to do basic household budgeting and make better financial choices. We are very clear and upfront with our clients from day one as to the importance of being on time with their rent/ housing payments. This not only helps create a positive track record for the client when it comes time for them to apply for a bank mortgage, it also helps with the "mindset shift" from renter to owner so that when that client does get that bank mortgage, they will be at a reduced risk of foreclosure down the road. Our clients have taught us, in most cases, it is not a lack of income that stops people on their quest to become homeowners, but rather a lack of knowledge and discipline as to how to make it happen. We are so fortunate to be able to impart knowledge to others that will help them fulfill their dreams!

Our philosophy is to not only increase value by showing our clients how to get into a home, but also educating them to make them experienced homeowners when we let them go. That's a very unique way of doing this real estate business. Most real estate investors operate from an all-for-self type of model, "buy a property, sell a property, make a lot of money." That's not what we want for the long term. We have a true passion to help people. Our 15+ years of experience, respectively in the medical profession, further supports our desire to care for others. Our goal is to leave those we work with better off than they were when they came to us. Being able to aid others in bettering their situation is what really appealed to us about the Path to Home Ownership® model. We pride ourselves in helping families and when we do that, we know more referrals will come our way, which is a win- win!

We love working with and for our home sellers. We are able to offer quick and flexible terms to buy properties. Our sellers come from all walks of life and circumstances. Sometimes there is an inherited property that the heirs no longer want to manage. There may be a marriage or even divorce for that matter where there are multiple properties involved and there becomes a need to liquidate a property. Retirees or empty nesters looking to downsize or relocate approach us for assistance with buying their properties. Home sellers who may find themselves like we once did, with negative equity and difficulty selling their property traditionally, find that we are able to offer several solutions to purchasing their property. Our sellers also are happy to learn that their property will be used by a deserving family with dreams of becoming homeowners. It does not matter what the situation is for our sellers, we are willing and able to assist.

It's important for us to help families on their journey to becoming homeowners because we know that homeownership improves the chance of financial success down the road. Being raised in a home that your parents actually own also lends itself to the children becoming more successful. We know that increasing home ownership has a direct relationship with increasing home property values. It also helps improve seemingly smaller, but no less important things like children being able to play freely, increased feelings of safety and security, and community building. People tend to take more pride in what they own; we know this to be true. We want to be a catalyst for change in the neighborhoods and communities in which we work. We want to be able to play a part in improving communities by creating more homeowners. We like to think that we are helping to build a legacy for the families that we help. A legacy that can be carried down through the generations.

Lastly, there is one more group of people that we provide a valuable service for, our private lenders. In order for our business to grow and to allow us to be able to acquire numerous properties so that we can continue to serve our clients, we depend on our network of individuals who lend us funds to do our deals. There are only so many transactions that can be done solely using our company's resources before all of our funds are occupied and therefore not available for doing future transactions. Traditional financial institutions, such as banks, will only lend a finite amount of money and write so many mortgages for a given person or entity. Furthermore, traditional bank financing for our business ventures is often too slow and cumbersome of a process, due to regulatory constraints placed on the financial sector, to be optimal as a primary option for funding. Our vision for helping individuals and families obtain home ownership is INFINITE. Therefore, we depend heavily on our network of regular everyday people looking to get a good return on funds currently not being put to work, (i.e. sitting in a bank account or under a mattress) or those with retirement funds looking to get consistent returns with significantly improved safety of their underlying principle. Unlike the volatility or risk found traditionally in the stock market, our private lenders benefit from getting respectable rates of return on their money, combined with the added safety of every investment they make with us being secured by an underlying asset. You see, we are all about doing good and at the same time doing well. We believe all parties involved should win.

Working with Lou Brown and the Path to Home Ownership® program has been a blessing for us. Not only has his program elevated our business and helped us to run it properly and successfully, but we have also had the opportunity to meet and network with some awesome people. Our nationwide CAHP- Certified Affordable Housing Provider® family has been incredibly supportive and full of innovative ideas. We are so glad to be a part of this group!

About Eddie and Valerie Coverson

Eddie grew up in and around Atlanta, GA and Valerie is from Jacksonville, FL. Eddie and Valerie met in college at Florida A&M University, where they studied physical therapy. After graduation, board exams and physical therapy practice, they married in 2004. Together they have 2 sons who they involve in the business more and more as they grow.

They are managing partners at Eagle Eye Home Solutions, LLC, established in 2016, and have continued to build the business, brand and credibility by becoming Certified Affordable Housing Providers® in 2016 as well. In addition, they have also earned the following certifications:

- Certified Income Specialist
- Certified Deal Specialist
- Certified Trust Specialist
- Master of Business Advancement Certification

Follow team Eagle Eye on Facebook @eagleeyehomesolutions and Twitter @eagleeyehomes

You can also visit team Eagle Eye at any time via the following websites:

If you're looking to sell property: **www.EagleEyeHouseBuyers.com**

If you're looking to rent or buy: **www.EagleEyeHomeSellers.com**

If you are interested in learning more about investing with us as a private lender, visit: **www.EagleEyeFunding.com**

678-435-0813

1-888-778-9008

Chapter 16

A Solution Provider

Jeanne Towne

"Committed to Excellence With Integrity!"

I first got started in real estate investing in the early 2000's. I started with a mentorship course with Angie Ryan and Claude (Financial Health Coach) in 2004, way before the crash. Nobody even knew what short sales were back then, so I had a great advantage. We were buying properties through the negotiated discount from banks, and I did very well.

I then started to take other Guru's courses, like Ron Legrand, Jeff Kaller Lou Brown, just to name a few. However, I seemed to resonate the best with Lou Brown. He has stamina in this business, and I loved the fact that he taught his own stuff. Plus, he is an awesome mentor as well as the founder of this movement!

I love to help people, and I love to create a good win-win situation. Short Sales are a good niche for this: The Banks win because they get paid, I win because I make money and the sellers get out of the debt problem that they were in. Being a Christian, I like to operate with integrity and make sure that people get taken care of properly. It's all about doing good while doing well. You can make rather good money while doing this, but you're ultimately helping people, you're helping the economy, you're helping the community by assisting to stabilize the housing crisis and we assist the home seller with their distressed situation. We also provide credit restoration to help our home buyers help themselves, so ultimately, they can refinance and enjoy homeownership that they can afford! This Certified Affordable Housing® program is just a no brainer for me. It's exactly right up my alley.

Doing Good While Doing Well

I am also incredibly blessed in the fact that my past brought me to my present. I have a degree in horticulture. I was a landscape contractor and designer for 30 years and worked with very high-end clients. As we got to know each other through my work they would have me do additional work besides just landscaping. So, I started subcontracting different jobs: pool resurfacing, decks, resurfacing driveways, screen patios, etc. I got to the point where I was subcontracting all these contractors. And one day the light bulb came on and I thought, *using my subcontractors, I could be buying and selling houses and doing this for myself. It's not like I don't know what I'm doing. It's in my blood!* Land developers go way back in my family, and I love to rehab houses. I know, it's probably not the best use of my investment money, but it's what works for me, and I enjoy doing it and seeing the finished product.

I'm very meticulous of the finishing touches. These are what makes the houses sell. Whether it's extra landscaping, higher end tile, focus walls, etc., you need to do what it takes to make your investment work for you. Since I pay such attention to the details, I often find myself getting my hands dirty tiling a backsplash, caulking some baseboard, touching up finishes or paint, etc. The small details make a huge difference. These little details are what sets me apart from other investors and their rehabs. It only takes a few rehabs to learn that you have to improve the property to the value level. I see a lot of new rehabbers that over-improve or under improve and they end up losing money and leave the business.

I like Lou Brown's theory about building stabilized residual income because that's one thing that I haven't done enough of. I do have some rental properties, but not enough. At my age I should have more! So, I like that theory, but there's also situations where they would not make a good buy and hold property. For instance – condos. Personally, I don't like to buy and hold condos because of the associations and what comes along with them. The owners are responsible for assessments and things like that, even though my buyers are responsible for those. It's just a high default area. And quite frankly, when I put somebody in a property, I want to try to keep them in that property. I don't want them to default. I'd rather just turn that property over. However, there are other properties that are great deals, need a bit of rehabbing and in the end we end up wholesaling it. I do that as well... wholesale, retail, buy and hold. I've got a whole tool bag that I can use. So for the seller, I can pretty much take a problem property and determine a good solution for it.

My biggest need and desire at this time is to work with more sellers. I feel that currently the economy is leading us more that way. Many want to downsize, upgrade, have a life-style change or try a different location and I am happy to help them with the next phase of their life. I am also a licensed realtor, so I also enjoy that aspect of the business. I can help them with getting top dollar for their sale. So, with just about every selling aspect, I have a solution. That's why I like to consider myself as a solution provider.

Looking to the Future

80% of the country already are unable to qualify for conventional loans and it's looking like that number will be rising. Somebody who qualified for a mortgage prior to losing their job no longer qualifies, because they have to have two years of consecutive employment. As Americans, we've kind of been convinced that you should buy the nicest house you can afford, which can be a big mistake for people. Much better to buy something that's more affordable, pay it off quick and then start to upgrade. So many of the young buyers want to buy a home like their parents and they forget it took their parents 30 years or more to get to that kind of knowledge.

I have hard money lenders that would qualify me with a quick phone call. But, I'm paying more money, more interest plus points to some of those investors. Therefore, private money is always a good tool to have, especially if you get an ongoing relationship with somebody like I have with some of my hard money lenders. They're begging me to borrow money because I've been in business for a long time and I don't default. I make sure there's enough of a cushion. And I think I've only lost money on One house and I've only broken even on One and the rest I've made profits on for the duration of my whole career. Most of that I have to contribute to education, such as looking at what other people have done wrong, what they didn't do, and what they did right.

The bottom line is that putting people in a home that they can't qualify for with a bank is huge for me because I have been in that situation. I've made good money, had a good income, didn't default on my payments, but my credit got damaged for one reason or another and nobody wanted to loan me money for a long time. Today, the people that do loan me money, loan me money on equity base. I used to do 30% skin in the game, and now I can do as little as 10%. The interest rates drop considerably, and they are begging me to borrow money. Their private lenders are always asking for me because I've established a good working relationship, <u>I don't default with them</u>, so now they're knocking at my door, throwing money at me. That's the way I want to be for my clients. I want to be able to provide housing for them that nobody else will provide. I also know darn well that they can make the payments and they appreciate it and they're doing good.

Giving someone an opportunity to get back on their feet again is my way of paying it forward. The *Path To Home Ownership*® program is the easiest way to do just that.

About Jeanne Towne

Jeanne Towne a S. Florida Realtor/Investor servicing the Broward and Monroe County Areas. She specializes in Distressed Properties, Short Sales and Waterfront properties. Service with integrity is her priority! Jeanne can make cash offers within 24 hours or will list a property and get the highest and best price for her client. Her expertise lies in the areas of marine and residential construction.

Jeanne has been working with short sales since 2004 and has extensive knowledge in this area. Her work ethics are to serve the public with honesty and integrity and assisting to achieve their Real Estate Goals utilizing her expertise and knowledge.

Jeanne has an extensive background buying and selling distressed properties since 2004. She has been remodeling houses, upgrading neighborhoods, and procuring a first-time home buyer a good deal with home warranties to get their start. She enjoys creating win/win situations. Jeanne was buying houses through negotiating short sale discounts for her investment properties and decided to get her Real Estate License and do the same for others.

Doing Good While Doing Well

Jeanne loves to help people and the Path To Home Ownership® program is very exciting to her as she can make a very serious impact in the community by providing the best win-win situations she has seen in many years. There are many facets to the world of Real Estate and because of the current glut of bank-owned properties that will be entering the market, Jeanne has decided to focus in this area. Her experience with Real Estate and different market conditions make Jeanne a No Nonsense Real Estate Expert!

Other areas of expertise include Jeanne being a licensed Realtor, Contractor, Short Sale Specialist, Landscape Designer, and Business Entrepreneur who operates with the upmost Integrity and considerers her ethical and moral standards to be the most important part of her career.

To learn more about how Jeanne can help you with your real estate needs, contact her directly at **(954) 317-5964** or visit her website at **www.LivingWaterHome.com** if you want to buy and **www.24HourHomeBuyer.com** if you want to sell.

Chapter 17

Solving Problems For Sellers & Buyers

Roy and Diana Cooper

"Success has nothing to do with what you gain in life or accomplish for yourself. It's what you do for others." ~ Danny Thomas~

I was into real estate at an early age. I bought my first duplex right after high school at the ripe young age of 18. Soon after, I bought my first tri-plex. Not long after that I met my wife and started our family. Now that our two boys are out on their own it's time to move on to the next phase of our lives.

During my junior and senior years in high school I attended a vocational school where I studied Heating, Air Conditioning & Refrigeration. Since then I worked in several different areas within home repair and maintenance industry. Soon after we were married I obtained additional education to allow me to transition into facility management.

Even though we've been buying some property in the Pittsburgh area over the years, I wanted to do more. When I heard about Lou's Street Smart® program I knew it was a great fit for us. So we hooked up with Lou and have been going strong and steady ever since. In our journey we have known many people in this business who are only in it to make a fast buck, to become a "real estate millionaire." That's not our goal. We are very blessed with what we have. Our goal is to give back, helping people obtain homeownership that really can't do it any other way. That's our drive for doing this business.

Diana is a nurse by trade but was also impressed with Lou's programs and decided to join in the business so that we both could do it full time while helping others. And we make a great team. When we have a homeowner interested in selling their property, Diana works with the individuals to determine their needs and how we can assist them in solving their problem. After Diana collects all of the details and she determines it's a win – win for both parties she sets up an appointment for me to see the property. After I determine the needed repairs and associated costs we evaluate the numbers and if the deal makes sense, she works with the owner throughout the buying process to procure the home. We also split other duties within the company, but we always cross-learn so that either one of us can do part of the other one's job if need be. It just makes good business sense.

To make the Path to Home Ownership® program really work for us we are always looking for excited buyers. We are looking to grow our number to at least another 20 properties this year. Listen, I'm 57 years old. We are financially comfortable. The extra income helps, but that's not the reason why we are doing this. It truly IS to help others. For instance, one of our clients, a handyman that was working with us, was having trouble with his landlord. But because of his circumstances he never thought he would be able to own his own home. Well, we helped him do just that. He was so grateful. He said, "No one has ever done anything like this for me." It touched us, and hits home as to the reason we are doing this.

We recently had an individual contact us about his sister's house as the executor of her estate. Since he had a home of his own, he had no desire to keep the property. The house needed many repairs and updates to sell it the traditional way. He did not have the time, money or interest in undertaking such a project. Diana negotiated all the details and we were able to purchase the house in a timely manner. The seller was so appreciative with the ease and simplicity of the process he recommended us to another seller. Following the Street Smart System® we were able to make the needed repairs and place a Path To Home

Ownership® client into the property shortly after closing. She is a single mother with three children living at home. After her divorce she was living with her older daughter and desired a home for her and her children.

Many of the people in our CAHPs program (Certified Affordable Housing Provider®) like ourselves, are motivated by wanting to help more and more people. Fortunately, we are getting excellent business training and exposure to other investors doing what we're doing that by generating a fair profit, it allows us to be in the position we are in of actually helping more and more people.

So, it's a good balance. And the more we do it, the easier it gets, which means we can help more people. And with our systems in place, it also affords us the opportunity to step away from the business for a few months, if needed, to recoup and regroup. Not many businesses allow for that kind of flexibility. Time and freedom, to our way of thinking, is important.

I want to say that I am not the type of person that is looking forward to retirement. I love to be doing and I love to be learning. That's why I find real estate so fascinating and rewarding. Even though it's a business, it's something that we can do at our leisure. When we are in the process of negotiating, sometimes it's easy for us to walk away from a deal if it's not to our liking. We don't have to think, *Oh my, I have to get this one so I can get the rehab loan and pay my rent.* That's a powerful position to be in.

I think that's true of most people in our organization. I feel that the fairer you are with the seller, the more properties you're going to get. But we also know that the better buys we get, the easier it is to help the buyer get into it. So it's a real balancing act. It's great when money is not the only determining factor as to whether we can do the deal or not.

Doing Good While Doing Well

But sometimes, to be honest, it's not always easy closing a deal. Not the deal itself but talking to the private money people about investing in the deal. We're lucky in the fact that we have a self-directed IRA that we use and one or two private lenders. But it's not easy going up to a stranger, or even people we know and asking them to fund us. It's a risk. We're still in the learning mode for that, as we know others are, so that is something that we are working on. But as time goes on I know we will get better at that. We just have to remember the bigger picture... no money, no house, no making someone's dream come true.

But no matter what, we try and make the best deal for everyone involved – the seller, the buyer and us. When we talk with our sellers, we let them know up front that it's got to be a win for them. Also, we just can't come in and lowball them and give them a number that's unrealistic. That's not going to solve their problem, and we're here to solve their problem. However, many times we will let them know about the perspective new owner. We will let them know about the family or the individual. We will let them know that without this deal, the perspective buyer may never have another opportunity to own their own home. We let them know that when they sell their house to us that they're going to be helping another individual obtain homeownership, so it's a win-win for everyone.

About Roy and Diana Cooper

Roy was born in Norfolk, Virginia and moved back to Pennsylvania after his father completed his service in the navy. Shortly after high school he started a heating and air conditioning business and obtained an associate degree from Penn State in Electrical Engineering. Roy also had a short stint in commercial real estate as an agent.

Diana was born in Glendale California, moved to Pennsylvania, then back to California during her high school years and ended up in nursing school in Sewickley, Pennsylvania. She continued her education at Waynesburg College where she obtained her bachelor's degree in nursing.

Roy and Diana met by chance and married in 1984. They have two boys, two grandsons and two granddaughters. As a couple they started investing in real estate in 2013. They are currently active members of Pittsburgh REIA, A+ members of the Better Business Bureau and continue with ongoing Street Smart® training. They have completed their training and are Certified Affordable Housing Providers® (CAHP).

Doing Good While Doing Well

To learn more about how Roy and Diana can help you with your housing needs, contact them directly at **agent@yourpahomesolution.com** or **412-353-3704**. You can also visit their websites at:

www.yourpahomesolution.com
www.sellyourpittsburghhousefast.com
www.ownapittsburghhome.com

Chapter 18

Leveling the Playing Field

By Roger Thomas

"Live..Love..Matter"
~ Brendon Burchard~

I spent 20+ years working in corporate America for a large marketing firm. While I did enjoy my work, I did not feel like it was what I really wanted to do with my life. In 2009 I bought a two-family house, lived upstairs and rented the downstairs. I really enjoyed that time and found that it was a great way to build passive income for my retirement. Through the years of getting to know my tenants, I started to see how difficult it was for most people to qualify for a loan to buy their own house. My tenants were all great people and deserved a chance at the American Dream of homeownership. A few years ago, I decided that helping good people attain home ownership was what I truly wanted to do with my career. Between working with my tenants, family, and friends, I knew this was something I could do to help people. It was while I was looking for a way to help them that I met Lou Brown. Through his programs and intense trainings and certifications, I became a *Certified Affordable Housing Provider®* (CAHP). I quickly learned that about 80% of the population can't qualify for conventional bank loans. So, this was a way that I could help people get their very own home, something that many have been dreaming about for years, while also helping my own family build up equity over time for our retirement.

Currently I am working to place people in as many homes as possible. I continue to look for multi-family units to purchase and use for my renters as we help them build up their credit and down-payment money. The goal is to get as many people as possible in our "Path To Home Ownership®" program and help them move up the levels from renting, to rent to own (Lease Option), then Agreement for Deed (Owner Financing), all the while working towards the end goal of traditional bank financing, which provides lower monthly payments. Members can come into the program at any level and can skip levels while working towards homeownership. Moving up levels requires improving their credit and building up a larger down payment. We help build a plan for each member tailored to their needs. We sit down with every member and go through their situation and what type of house they are looking for and we help figure out how much they can comfortably afford for monthly house payments. On top of this, we know that most people actually don't understand finances and credit. With the people that we're working with, it's not just getting them into a home; it's helping them to understand and rebuild their credit. We help by reporting their rent payments to the credit bureaus, which helps build up their credit. We also work with them on budgeting and helping them to realize what it takes to maintain a property. Since many have been renters for most of their lives, they don't understand about the upkeep. It takes money to fix issues. Before, the landlord did it. Now the ball is in their court, and we show them how to put money aside for when these issues arise. We're an all-in-one service to help people not only get their perfect home but learn how to take care of it and keep it for the long term.

We also strive to help homeowners that need or want to sell their property. There are a lot of investors out there trying to buy properties. Most see each property and owner as a number and simply fire off a quick cash offer. We are different in that we take the time to get to know the owner and understand what is truly important to them. A lot of times, the owner doesn't want to sell. In this case, we do everything we can to help them keep the house. We know this means we won't be able to buy that property, but we will have helped someone, and that is what is most important to us. We believe that good faith will come back to us down the road. In other cases, someone might need cash right away, so a cash offer will work best. Some might not have the time or money to fix up the property so it can be listed with an agent, or they simply don't want to wait the approximate 4 – 6 months it takes to close on a listed property. Other owners are not good with money or may be retiring and looking to downsize. In these cases, what might be best for them is some money now and monthly payments they can live off of going forward. We also work with people in foreclosure or who have inherited a property from the loss of a loved one. These people need someone to help them understand the process, walk them through it, and be sympathetic to the situation they are dealing with. Then, if there is a property that needs to be sold, we can potentially help them with that. We have specialized members of our team for both Foreclosures and Probate leads for this reason.

In the case of Probate leads, we offer at no charge a full program helping people through each step of the process on an inherited property. We have a team in place to help remove items from the home, assist in an estate sale for any items of value, introduce them to an attorney and financial planner to assist with the paperwork and financial planning for the remaining assets and money, and bring in a real estate agent if the property is in good shape and can be listed. When there is a property involved, we can help them fix it up and sell at retail, or if they just want to get rid of it or need the money to potentially use for another home, we will purchase it and put one of our families into the property. We would then fix-up the house, or our future owner would do the work as part of the work for equity program we offer, which would then count towards their down payment.

I live in Connecticut and primarily work in five counties: Harford, Middlesex, New London, Tolland, and Windham, although we do work with people all across the state. Connecticut is a small state, so it's very easy for us to work state-wide. But we are particular about the houses that we purchase. We choose the neighborhoods carefully, making sure they are a good fit for our clients. With our multi-families, we look for units in the $150,000 to $300,000 range. We also look for single-family houses mostly in working-class neighborhoods, where a good starter home would typically cost around the $150,000 to $225,000 range. We're not opposed to lower or higher homes, but these price ranges are our comfort zones.

Now on the investing side, we are always looking for private investors at any price point. So if someone has less than $50,000 but wants to invest it, we will use that for rehab projects and purchase down payments. If somebody has more than $50,000, whether it's an IRA or cash, we would use that to acquire properties, or for the rehab, if needed. To make the deals as enticing as possible, we typically pay investors a set interest rate of anywhere from 5% to 8%, depending on the deal and the investor. We are also open to equity partners on some larger projects. There are not a lot of safe options out there for people to receive a good return on their investment. Bank savings accounts and CDS barely pay 1%. For a lot of other people, dealing with the uncertainty of the stock market is not appealing. We have all heard too many stories of hard-working people losing all of their retirement savings to a stock market crash. This is where Real Estate is different. Now, home values can drop, but you never see the value of a property drop by 80% overnight like you can with stocks. This is also where experience and high-level training comes into play. We look at every property and have multiple ways to buy as well as exit the deal. We run the numbers conservatively, taking into account the possibility of a market shift and home prices dropping. With stocks, funds, and bonds, you have a piece of paper that says you own something. With Real Estate, you are more protected as you have a tangible asset. If we purchase the home with a private investor's money, they hold the mortgage in their name and are on the insurance policy so if something happens and we don't make the payments, they can easily get the property back to cover their investment.

People like that we are a family-run business and that our mission is to help both sellers and buyers to create a situation where we can help everyone involved. Our goal is to continue to grow throughout the state and then open offices in other states as well. Our primary focus has always been to help the public and to get people into homes. It's getting harder and harder to get qualified by the banks, which is why the *Path To Home Ownership®* program is needed. So our focus is just to try to help as many people as possible, hence, *Doing Good While Doing Well™*. We take time each day to appreciate how blessed we are to be in the position to help others.

Our 10-year goal is to start the Skawinski Foundation in honor of my parents. The foundation will have two specific goals:

- ✓ First, each year we will select a high school graduate from our Alma Mater that is not necessarily meant to go to college. We will select an individual with an entrepreneurial mindset looking to build their own future. We will provide hands-on mentoring, access to education and training, as well as funds to start or grow a business they develop, whether it has to do with real estate investing or not.
- ✓ The second mission is still to be ironed out but will involve helping children in some capacity. We are still determining if we will team up with local programs to assist children in hospitals, assist single-parent families, or potentially provide teaching and experiences to underprivileged children.

This is how WE level the playing field!

About Roger Thomas

Roger Thomas worked in the Promotional Marketing Industry for 20+ years, managing IT & Creative Service Teams as well as the RFP process and presentations to many Fortune 500 companies over the years.

Roger was born in Hartford, Connecticut and grew up in Colchester, Connecticut. He currently resides in Glastonbury, Connecticut, with his beautiful family. Roger's better half, Christy, works for Hartford Health Care and continues to take on a more active role in the company. They are blessed with two beautiful children, Zack & Samantha. Their goal is to provide their children with options and the attitude that anything is possible with dedication and persistence.

Outside of Real Estate, Roger enjoys spending as much time with his family as possible, golfing, nature, and the company of good friends.

For more information on Paradigm Homes East, please reach out to Roger at: **roger@paradigmhomeseast.com**

For homeowners looking to sell their property, please check out their website at: **www.ParadigmHomesEast.com**

For People interested in becoming a member of the Path To Home Ownership® program, please check out: **www.Rent2owninCT.com**

For anyone looking for a better, safer way to invest their money with steady, safe returns, please visit them at: **www.InvestWithPHE.com**

Chapter 19

A Service Calling – Homeland Properties

Joe and Patty Peltier

"If you light a lamp for someone else, it will also brighten your path."
~Budda~

I am what is colloquially known as a "military brat." That is to say that I was raised in a military family. My father was in the Air Force. His father was in the Army. Many of my relatives also served in the military at one time or another. So, when I came of age, my first "productive" move was to join the military to get my head straight because frankly, I wasn't doing well, and the rigor and discipline of the culture felt like home. Thanks, teenager years!

I also felt compelled to do something for my country. I knew what fighting for my country meant, I knew what our freedom meant, and I wanted to make sure that I ensured all of the good things that come with those commitments were preserved for the next generation. So, after a year or two of failed attempts at college, I joined the Army. I didn't know it at the time, but in that one decision I changed who I was and would become forever. It turned into a 20 year career where I began as an enlisted Private, then "bootstrapped" up to become an officer and leader of soldiers. Those 20 years saw the completion of not only my undergraduate, but also my master's degree and my becoming the head of my own family with my wife, Patty, and our five children joining the team along the way

We decided that 2013 would mark my last year in the service; I retired and we moved the family to one of our past duty stations in San Antonio, Texas. They call it Military City, USA. It's a very nice area, very military friendly and had been one of our duty stations during my time in the

137

service - so not only did we already own property there, we were also very familiar with the area. Soon after establishing in town we bought another house and moved to the outskirts of San Antonio on almost 21 acres to be closer to my parents and give our family room to grow. It was also something that Patty was more comfortable with, having grown up in the rural areas of the west coast of Florida.

It took about a year for us to figure out that while retirement pay was good, we were doing okay, but the kids were starting to come of age and they would be starting college soon. As we looked ahead I said, "Well, I'm not going to be able to afford that. I need to figure out what the future is going to look like now." Somewhere along the line we found real estate investing, holding long-term properties and renting them as a stream of income. It wasn't long before we'd bought enough properties that we couldn't qualify for loans without a source of W2 income. That led to me starting a second career, in line with my mentoring/coaching background, helping college students navigate through their degree program with Western Governors University.

All of this is to say, we stumbled and bumbled our way through real estate investing before finding a good mentor. Lou Brown showed us the right way to do it.

The 'persistent theme' to my whole life seems to be centered around making mistakes, learning from them, then helping other people not to make them: guiding, mentoring, and coaching. Helping other people is a natural fit for Lou's program.

Our very first deal was a house that I found through a realtor in another program. The specific focus of this program is to buy a distressed property, usually right out of the MLS. Buy distressed, fix it up and then put a tenant into it.

So, it was pretty simple, right?

Well, this property was really in bad shape. We had more time than money at the time so I actually did the work on it myself to get it up t to where we could have tenants living in it. Then after finding tenants, our work still wasn't done. We were having all the typical headaches of a landlord. Folks really didn't care about the place so they didn't keep it up. Honestly, it would have been good if it came out as advertised. You know, you just fix it up and everybody lives up to their goals and aspirations in life and pays the rent on time and doesn't damage the place. Maybe in a parallel universe! We still have that property but now, with Lou's coaching, we've expanded the company and are working with the right clients, people that want to do the right thing... they want to do things the right way and help us to help them. That's where the *Path To Home Ownership®* program comes in to play.

With the *Path To Home Ownership®* we can help the underserved in our community by meeting them where they are, in terms of income and credit worthiness, then place them into a home of their choosing to be their forever home. This is the ultimate win-win! We help them become home owners and they help us with a destination, an end state for our real estate assets. Each step along the way we get to coach, guide and mentor our future 'home owners in training'.

CAHP Positive

What really excited us about becoming CAHPs, Certified Affordable Housing Providers®, was the entire structure of Lou's program. It's soup to nuts... all put together. It all makes sense. From getting started with a property all the way through what you do with the property after you have it to what it's going to turn into. You pretty much know all that right from the beginning. With the CAHP program we are able to let people know that we're here to serve and bring deserving folks into those properties in a way that just wasn't there before.

Even better, we're not alone. There are other CAHPs here in San Antonio, which is how we initially found Lou in the first place. We ran into a CAHP at an Equity Trust class at the local REIA and when we got together a little later and the whole program was explained it was a natural fit ÷ Lou's been our mentor and our local "guy on the ground" as far as figuring out problems and sharing resources.

Our number one goal is to retire Patty, bring her onboard full-time and make this a true family business by bringing in the kids as well. Patty has been working for many years as a contract employee on the Air Force Base doing refractive surgery for the soldiers and airmen. She is also in the mindset of helping our community and shares the servant's calling. While her role is currently limited by her job to maintaining our records, she's also looking forward to staging properties, getting them ready for new clients and then eventually growing into being our sales/leasing agent.

We both look forward to that day.

About Joe and Patty Peltier

Joe Peltier enlisted in the Army in 1991 and graduated with Honors with a Bachelor of Science in International Studies from the University of Tampa. Joe was commissioned into the Armor branch of the Army in 1998 when Patty joined the team. Patty Peltier, a native Floridian, had been serving the community as a Certified Ophthalmic Technician since 1988. In 2001, Joe was branch transferred to Military Intelligence where he spent the rest of his career training, developing, coaching and mentoring soldiers.

Together Joe and Patty traveled stateside and abroad over Joe's remaining military career including assignments together and apart as Joe was called to duty and deployments in such diverse locations as Germany, Korea, Japan, Iraq, Afghanistan, Greece and Africa. Before retiring in 2013, Joe earned a Master of Business Administration, Human Resources Management degree from the University of Phoenix; then earned a Project Management Professional certification from the Project Management Institute.

Since opening the doors to their real estate investing business in San Antonio in 2014, Joe and Patty have served 12 families and hundreds of visitors from around the world with short-term rental offerings. Under the Street Smart System®, Joe has earned recognition as a Certified Affordable Housing Provider®, Certified Deal Specialist, Certified Income Specialist and will be completing the requirements for Trust Specialist Certification this fall. Together, Joe and Patty look forward to their first submission to the GD Sanford Foundation by mid-2020 for recognition with the Community Affordable Housing Provider Award.

We are ardent supporters of the *Path To Home Ownership®️ Movement.* For more information about how we can serve you and/or assist on your *Path To Home Ownership®️* read more about Homeland Properties' services to the San Antonio community at:

www.sahomelandproperties.com

www.alamocitypropertybuyers.com

www.homelandcapitalfunds.com

Chapter 20

Because I Said "Yes"

By Janice Brown

"Do or Do Not.. There is No Try" ~ Yoda~

I married into real estate. My parents were homeowners but not investors. I wasn't interested in real estate and had no concept about what it entailed, how to do it, or even why anyone would be interested. When I left college, my plan was to change the world through social work.

That didn't turn out so well.

First there were, at that time, no jobs available in social work. I guess I was not the only person who left college, figuring they could fix the world. Second, government didn't seem to have the money for new positions or new ideas. Third, I discovered the world didn't really want to be fixed – even with my great ideas. So, I got a job in retail management because the company needed women managers. I discovered new worlds for my social work experience. I discovered that social work is actually a good foundation for managing people.

It was while working in retail that I met and married Lou. This was also when I met real estate for the first time as an intimate part of my life. Where Lou is, so there dwells real estate. He went to seminars and read books. I didn't. He bought courses and studied. I didn't.

He bought more courses and went to more seminars. I didn't. He faithfully attended the monthly real estate association meetings. I didn't. Lou began his career as a full-time real estate investor just after our daughter and second child Diana was born. I went to work at a job as a medical social worker. He volunteered and then became a Board member at the local real estate investors association. I did go to the picnics with Lou and the kids. He became a member of RELAA. I couldn't remember what that stood for. He transformed it into National REIA. I thought that was a good idea because then I could remember what it meant and the discounts he planned for the memberships sounded really good for us. The whole point is real estate was Lou's thing. I really didn't consider it as that big a part of my little world until Lou and I talked about Lou going into real estate investing full time. That caught my attention.

We talked about it. A lot. We had sold one business and his staying self-employed didn't upset me. We talked about the money that would be involved and the time and the energy. I supported it because I knew Lou loved real estate investing and he would be good at it. I had no idea where that simple agreement would take me.

My job as a medical social worker gave us some income and most especially it provided health insurance for us and our kids. Real estate impinged on my life in odd ways. We would cruise his neighborhoods on our way home from church and sometimes looked at houses. Some weekends we would spend cleaning a house to get it ready for a new tenant. The kids even worked, too, and earned some spending money. At some houses toys would be left and for those we got an amazing amount of work out of a 4 and 5-year-old. He spent a ton of time volunteering and building GaREIA (Georgia Real Estate Investors Association) and then National REIA. Occasionally, I would type letters or contracts. I still remember typing my first legal description. I am dyslexic and that paragraph of feet and directions and turns and degrees was a nightmare.

Then our kids got old enough to start school. And I wanted to be home for that.

So Lou and I had another talk about how our life could look should I decided to leave my good job and stay home. Lou offered me this fabulous part-time, temporary job. I would do the paperwork and answer the phone and look through the ads in the paper and just assist Lou. This sounded good to me and I took the job.

Then Lou gave me my first contract to do.

As far as I was concerned, it was a blank sheet of paper. Three blank sheets of paper. I had no relationship with it. I had second thoughts about this fabulous part-time job.

However, we persevered and got through that and learned how to work together and started an amazing journey together that has resulted in a business that not only pays the bills but allows us to help others and contribute to our community.

I evolved into being in full-time charge of our property management. There are things about my job that can drive me totally crazy. They're called tenants.....wait, no, clients. My clients can make me unbalanced at times. The phone ringing off the hook can become irritating. The water department, code enforcement, trashed houses, court, trying to get employers and previous landlords to call me back, getting contractors into tenanted houses to do repairs...I could name a few more dozen things that can get me going.

You know what makes it worth everything? It's not just the money coming in.

It's the feeling I get when I KNOW I've put the right family in the right house. It's the feeling that I made a difference in someone's life who never dreamed they could own their own house. It's driving down a street in a neighborhood where we've renovated several houses and seeing how the neighborhood has changed. That's happened to me many times now. It's just a great feeling.

It's Leon that makes it all worthwhile. He's 63 and never owned his own home. He's been in his home now for 9 months. He's still amazed it's happening. His son called me because he wants the same deal. We're looking for a house for him now. So far nothing has fit, but the right house is coming. Leon moved into his house and did our 'Work For Equity' program. The down payment credit he earned is more than he will need and Leon is getting together his paperwork to apply for a bank loan. He loves to show what he did to his house, not just the work for equity work, but what he and his wife did to make that house their very own. They'd never been able to choose their own paint colors before.

It's Tara Bell that makes it all worthwhile. She's a single nurse who wanted her own home but didn't know how she could afford it. She did the work for equity program as well and sent us pictures of her dream kitchen when she got it done. Her kitchen island is a work of art. She exercised her option, stepped up, and is now a Gold level member. I've urged her to take that last step, but she's more comfortable staying with us, she says.

It's people like Willie and his wife that make it all worthwhile. They walked into the office and asked me if I had a house for rent. Willie said he wanted to be upfront with me and told me they had been dispossessed in the past. They looked beaten down and hopeless. I told them that if I had a house that rented for 1/3 of their monthly income and they would agree to payroll deduction, I could rent them a home. I don't think they really believed me but put in their applications anyway. I sent them to two houses and they fell in love with one. Willie painted the house inside and out and also put in a privacy fence. By the time they had moved in and lived there for two months, they didn't look like the same people. That's the difference a home can make.

It's Miss Mary that makes it worthwhile. Miss Mary came in to apply for a house for herself and her 15-year-old son. She wanted a better place to raise him than an apartment. She was concerned she didn't have enough money to buy, but after we went over the path to ownership, she was convinced she could. And excited about it. Her son wanted nothing else for Christmas but their house. Their whole Christmas was moving into THEIR house.

It's people like Carolyn and her husband that make it all worthwhile. She came into the office to talk to me and went to see nearly every house I had available in inventory. It took weeks for her to make a decision. What I didn't know was she was having a difficult time getting her husband to believe we would work with them on getting them into their own home. He kept telling her since he was self- employed they'd never get a loan. He kept reminding her we could be a scam. He told her they didn't have enough money saved and they would have to wait a while. When she told him about the Work For Equity Program, he finally called me. After we finished talking, he and Carolyn decided on a 4 bedroom home where he did the painting inside and out and installed the new a/c unit as he is an HVAC guy. The house is the one Carolyn went to see every week. They are very happy with their new home and I am very popular in their family.

It's people like Deirdre who make it worthwhile. Deirdre came to the office after a friend of hers told her about our program. Deirdre had just inherited 4 children and desperately needed to move from her 2 bedroom apartment into a house that would accommodate her new children, plus her other one, and her. We went through the inventory since she needed to move immediately. I had the perfect house already in inventory and move-in ready. Deirdre wanted a large kitchen so the kids could do homework while she worked in the kitchen and her house has that and a lot more that she wanted. Plus she needed a house the

social worker would approve of and her house is a home the social worker approved. The kids like living with their aunt. That's the difference the right home can make.

Doing Good While Doing Well

As for family, it's hearing my 17-year-old son say thank you because he had just seen the Great Pyramid. It's sitting on a wall in Machu Picchu and remembering my twin and I planning a trip to Peru just for Machu Picchu. It's watching my nine-year-old daughter's face when the guide at Tulum told her Mayan dancers got paid in chocolate but got killed if they made mistakes. It's walking around Ayers Rock with my dad after his telling me for decades he was on his way to Australia. It's talking with Lou's aunt in Edinburgh, Scotland about her speaking with Princess Diana the day the Princess visited the school she cooked at and watching Lou and his newfound cousin discuss nefarious plots they could have done had they known each other as boys. It's seeing my foster daughter on the Grand Staircase on a cruise ship and realizing her mother would love that picture and making sure her mother got it. All of those moments and more that enrich our family's lives are what makes it worthwhile to be in real estate investing.

What makes every day worthwhile is our conviction that not only are we helping people by providing them the opportunity of homeownership, but knowing we stabilize neighborhoods as owners (and those planning to be) are more invested in their homes and neighborhoods than renters. What makes every day worthwhile is the funds we can donate to the charities we feel make a huge difference in our communities. I feel it is a privilege to work in a business that allows us to enjoy life as well as helping people and communities while we do so. It is FUN to help people realize their dreams.

And to think all this came about because I had the intelligence to say yes when Lou asked me to marry him. I don't even want to think about what life might be like if we had never created a family and a business like this together. We are truly blessed!

About Janice Brown

Janice was born in Kentucky and raised in Texas, Florida and Kentucky. Her father graduated with his doctorate when she was ten. Her mother dropped out of college when she was a freshman and she was a sophomore because German was beyond her and she called the health class teacher an idiot because she got twins out of the rhythm method and wasn't going to let one child lie to babies about the facts of life. Janice is an identical twin and yes, she had fun with that when they were kids.

Janice graduated with a BA in sociology and psychology with a minor in juvenile law enforcement. She is also within 4 hours of completing her Master's degree in social psychology. She has worked as a juvenile high-risk youth center manager, a manager in retail merchandising, a medical social worker, and a property manager. She never bought a house and is not an investor. Janice manages, sells, rents, leases, and leases to own property.

Janice got into property management through marriage. She married Lou Brown in a moment of sheer brilliance without knowing what she was getting into by marrying him. She has traveled to Europe, Asia, Africa, South America, Central America, Australia, and New Zealand and driven through a lot of the USA. She has seen the Grand Canyon, the

Doing Good While Doing Well

Great Wall, Machu Picchu, Uluulu (Ayers Rock), the Pyramids, Jerusalem, waded in the Atlantic in Florida and in the Atlantic in Nigeria, danced with a blue-footed booby in the Galapagos Islands, and visited the Great Barrier Reef. She has seen cathedrals and castles all over Europe and stood in the Parthenon in Athens. She's walked in Trafalgar Square, Tiananmen Square, and Times Square. She's walked along the Seine, the Yangtze, the Mississippi, the Nile, and the Hudson rivers. She's boated down the Rhine River and would love to boat down the Amazon.

Janice has watched two children grow into amazing adults and a foster daughter find her place in the world. During all that she watched an amazing man teach himself the art of investing and the science of building a business and then proceed to develop systems to train and share an amazing business opportunity with thousands of other people.

Janice is thankful she had the sense to marry him.

Made in the USA
Columbia, SC
15 March 2024

32863843R00087